THE BIBLE STUDY

A One Year Study of the Bible and How It Relates to You

ISBN 978-0-9984910-1-1

For Worldwide Distribution

Printed in China

Words by Zach Windahl

Design by Zach Windahl and Katlyn Hovland

Web: www.thebrandsunday.com

Email: zach@thebrandsunday.com

Instagram: @zachwindahl

SHOUT OUTS

Pete and T. Windahl (aka mom and dad) for always inspiring me to chase my dreams, loving me so well, spending countless hours helping with this study, and for being my voice of reason.

Paul Weaver, Zach Shea, Daniel Okon, Austin Haugen, Alex Houg, and Antonio Sundquist aka the entire Activ team for helping take this thing to another level. You guys are insanely talented.

Scott and Kelly McClintock, Jesse Roberson, Justin Satterberg, and Alex Kruse for testing out the content and allowing me to bounce my crazy ideas off of you.

Chelsie, Lauren, Sarah, Kayla, Diana, Shea, Anna, mom, Jillaine, and Isabel for either modeling or allowing me to include your photos/artwork.

Katlyn Hovland for making me look way cooler than I actually am.

Brett and Sheila Waldman for answering my questions as I pursued printing/self-publishing and for partnering with me on product fulfillment.

Bryan Hunsberger, the staff, and all of the students from my time in Australia. Each and every one of you impacted my life more than you will ever know and for that I am forever grateful.

Luke Aslesen, Wade Branch, Caleb Cruse, and Ethan Salau for always being such good friends.

And finally, shout out to YOU for helping make this dream a reality.

INTRODUCTION

WELCOME TO THE BIBLE STUDY

Hopefully you have been with us from the beginning, but if you are just joining in then I will share my story and a little background of The Bible Study with you. If you did the Old Testament with us then you can skip this section.

I know that God aligned our paths on purpose, and I couldn't be more excited about what He is going to do in your life during this year-long journey together through the Bible.

My prayer is not only for you to have a better understanding of the Word, but that you will also find a better sense of meaning for your life and really understand the heart of our Father. He loves you SO much. It's amazing.

Before we dive into Genesis I want to share a little bit about my testimony. Who knows, you and I might even share some things in common. We're in this thing called life together. Let's go!

MY SEARCH FOR MEANING

Identity.
It's what makes you...you.

For many of us it takes years to figure out who we are and what we want to be. For some it comes easy, for others it takes a lifetime.

We have society, parents, teachers, friends, siblings, girlfriends, boyfriends, all telling us how we should live and act.

Why is it so easy for them to see it, but so difficult for us to figure it out?

If you're like me, I spent years trying to be the person that everyone else wanted me to be. Growing up, people would constantly tell me that I was going to be famous some day and that I should do this or that with my life. It all came from the fact that I was an entrepreneur from an early age and had a pretty unhealthy work ethic to back it. But it didn't matter how unhealthy that work ethic was because I was going to be FAMOUS some day and be seen with the elite. Or at least that's what I was told.

So my head grew.
And grew. And grew.
And grew.

I believed the hype and did all that I could to live it.

You see, I'm a product of my society. I'm a Bachelor's Degree graduate with $70k in debt from a Christian University that did anything but spark my interest in God, it actually pushed me farther away. Little did I know that the darkness inside of me at the time didn't like the Light inside of the students. Funny how that happens. So, after graduating, I had quite a bad taste in my mouth.

But, I kept talking the talk. I wrote two Christian books my senior year, but didn't have the nerve to promote them like I should have since I didn't even believe what was coming out of my mouth. I went on to run a clothing line and recording studio with some friends, which I left after a few years. I worked on some other entrepreneurial projects after that, but the hard work that I was putting into them was not lining up with the success (or lack thereof). Everything that I touched began to fail. I was "good" though. Or at least that's what I told myself.

In reality, I had no direction for where to go from there. I remember sitting in my car outside of Starbucks talking to my buddy Geoff about it. I had never felt so lost in my life. If you know me, you know I always have a plan. But this time I didn't. I was at the bottom. Broken and lost. I had spent the last several years focusing on myself and trying to become the best person I could be. But, to tell you the truth, I'm weak when I try to live life on my own. From the outside, everything looked great but the inside was a whole different story. Even though I thought I was "the man", I was still lacking something. My pride was fully intact, but my heart desired more.

I started to contemplate what all of this was about. I grew up considering myself a Christian, but I had no idea what that truly meant. I hadn't been following God's call at all. I still believed in Him, I just wasn't pursuing Him. I hadn't been to church in over a year for the simple fact that I couldn't stand the majority of Christians that I met because I didn't trust them. They all seemed so fake. So I sat there thinking…

Is life really all about going to college, getting a job, getting married, having kids, buying new things, and then (hopefully) one day retiring so I can enjoy life?

Really? That's it?
That all seemed so shallow to me.

Then, let's look at religion. Every religion outside of Christianity takes their faith so seriously, it's insane. And then there's us. Where only 30% of Christians even read the Bible and the fact that a ton of "Christian" ideals are pretty skewed from the Bible itself. I was fed up. So I read the Bible. Front to back. In 90 days.

I was blown away by how different the Bible actually is, compared to how it's presented in America. But that's what makes us Christians, right? The fact that we believe and follow Jesus?

Nothing was lining up. I was confused.

So I went on my own "Search for Meaning" journey. I quit my job and moved to a little beach town on the Sunshine Coast of Australia for 9 months to study the Bible for twelve hours a day. That's a pretty big leap if you ask me. And at 27 years old it may not have been the wisest of decisions, but I wouldn't have changed it for anything.

My whole reason for this journey was to build a firm foundation in my faith - one that could not be crumbled by society. And that's exactly what I got, plus more.

And that's what my hope is for you. That you are able to build a firm foundation in your faith over the next year. Especially in a time when understanding the Word is one of the most important things that you can do.

YOUR SEARCH FOR MEANING

It doesn't matter what you have done in the past. What matters is now. God loves you SO much and is SO delighted that you want to spend time getting to know Him through Scripture.

With all of that said, what are you hoping to get out of this year long study?

THE LAYOUT

The Bible Study is a year-long journey through the Word of God. All you need is this workbook and a Bible. The content is suitable for any believer, no matter what age or depth of your relationship with Jesus you have, it's for you.

Every week you will be studying 1-3 books of the Bible, depending on their size. Don't worry, I spaced them out so that it's manageable. You can see the suggested "One Year Study Plan" on the next page. Note that it's a little different than the layout of your Bible because it's more chronological to help you put a timeframe to things.

Weekly Rundown:

At the beginning of the week, you will read the first page from the workbook in order to get the basics of what you're about to dive into.

During the week, you will read the selected book(s) for that week at your own pace, ranging anywhere from 1-4 hours of reading time.

That's it! That's all I got for you. Enjoy your first book!

Z

P.S. Just like you, I want to know truth so I spend a lot of my time soaking in the Word of God and researching views of scholarly believers around the world. I love studying, really. It brings me to life. With that said, this study is a collaboration of material that I have gathered over the last few years and translated into modern-day terms to help better your understanding of the text (and mine). I am by no means an expert or a scholar. I just love helping people further their faith in Jesus Christ, our Lord and Savior.

ONE YEAR

STUDY PLAN

STUDY PLAN

FOUR MONTHS

27 BOOKS

9 AUTHORS

FIRST CENTURY AD

NEW

testament

M A T T H E W — R E V E L A T I O N

GOSPELS

Matthew

Mark

Luke

John

ACTS

Acts

PAULINE EPISTLES

Romans

1 Corinthians

2 Corinthians

Galatians

Ephesians

Philippians

Colossians

1 Thessalonians

2 Thessalonians

1 Timothy

2 Timothy

Titus

Philemon

HEBREW CHRISTIAN EPISTLES

Hebrews

James

1 Peter

2 Peter

1 John

2 John

3 John

Jude

REVELATION

Revelation

BOOKS & DATES

The Gospel of Matthew – AD 50-55

The Gospel of Mark – AD 55-60 or 64-68

The Gospel of Luke – AD 58-62

The Gospel of John – AD 80's

Acts – AD 60-62

Romans – AD 55-56

1 Corinthians – AD 55-56

2 Corinthians – AD 56

Galatians – AD 48 or 55

Ephesians – AD 60-61

Philippians – AD 60-61

Colossians – AD 60-61

1 Thessalonians – AD 50-51

2 Thessalonians – AD 50-51

1 Timothy – AD 64-66

2 Timothy – AD 67

Titus – AD 64-66

Philemon – AD 60-61

Hebrews – AD 64-65

James – AD 47-48 or 60-62

1 Peter – AD 64

2 Peter – AD 66

Letters of John – AD 90-95

Jude – AD 67-69

Revelation – AD mid-90's

As the common saying goes, "The New is in the Old concealed, but the Old is in the New revealed". The New Testament shows us how the Old Testament has been fulfilled through the life of Jesus, and shows us our current/future hope through the teachings of the epistles or letters.

The New Testament kicks off with the five historical books regarding Jesus and the early church, followed up by 14 of Paul's epistles, 7 Hebrew Christian epistles, and the book of Revelation. All of these books were written in Greek because that was one of the common languages and the writers all used the Greek version of the Old Testament (the Septuagint, LXX) in their studies.

KEY CHARACTERS

John the Baptist

John the Baptist was the final prophet of the Old Testament who arose after the 400 years of silence that followed the words of Malachi. He was the forerunner of Christ that was to pave the way and prepare the people for Jesus' arrival.

Jesus

God in the flesh. No need to explain. If you believe what he says, it changes everything.

Disciples

The word "disciple" means, "a follower or student of a teacher, leader, or philosopher" (oxforddictionaries.com). When we talk about the disciples of Jesus, we refer to his twelve closest friends while on Earth. They were Andrew, Bartholomew, James Son of Zebedee, James Son of Alphaeus, John, Judas Iscariot, Jude the brother of James, Matthew, Peter, Philip, Simon the Zealot, and Thomas.

Paul

Paul was known as a Hebrew of Hebrews, having studied under the great Gamaliel and was an extreme Pharisee by nature. Paul experienced a radical conversion to Christ (which we will read about in the book of Acts), and he became the greatest missionary of the early Church. Paul founded many churches around the Greco-Roman world, and today we have letters to some of those churches that give us the groundwork for our theology.

OVERVIEW

John

John was known as the "Beloved Disciple" because of how much Jesus loved him. He was faithful until the end and was entrusted with taking care of Mary, the mother of Jesus. He wrote one of the Gospels, three letters to his churches in Asia Minor, and the book of Revelation.

Luke

Luke was a physician that partnered with Paul during a portion of his missionary work. He was also the author of a Gospel and the book of Acts, which were both used as testimonies in Paul's Roman trial.

Peter

Peter was the first disciple that Jesus called to follow him. Jesus knew that he would be a great voice for the Kingdom so he changed his name from Simon (meaning "reed") to Peter (meaning "rock") and claimed that the Church would be built upon him. Peter had his ups and downs, but remained faithful to the end. He also gave us some amazing words recorded in his sermon on the day of Pentecost and in his two follow-up epistles.

James

James was a brother of Jesus that didn't believe Jesus was the Messiah until after his resurrection. James then became one of the top leaders for the church in Jerusalem and was highly respected among other believers. He ended up writing the book of James as "wisdom literature" to be added to the New Testament. It has been told that after he was martyred, his friends saw his knees for the first time and they were like the knees of camels from spending so much time in prayer.

Timothy

Timothy was Paul's spiritual son and was greatly loved by Paul himself. He also helped write a few of Paul's letters and had two letters written to him by Paul as encouragement to stand strong in the faith and continue on with the gospel message.

MID-STUDY THOUGHTS

What are you looking forward to the most about studying the New Testament after spending so much time in the Old Testament?

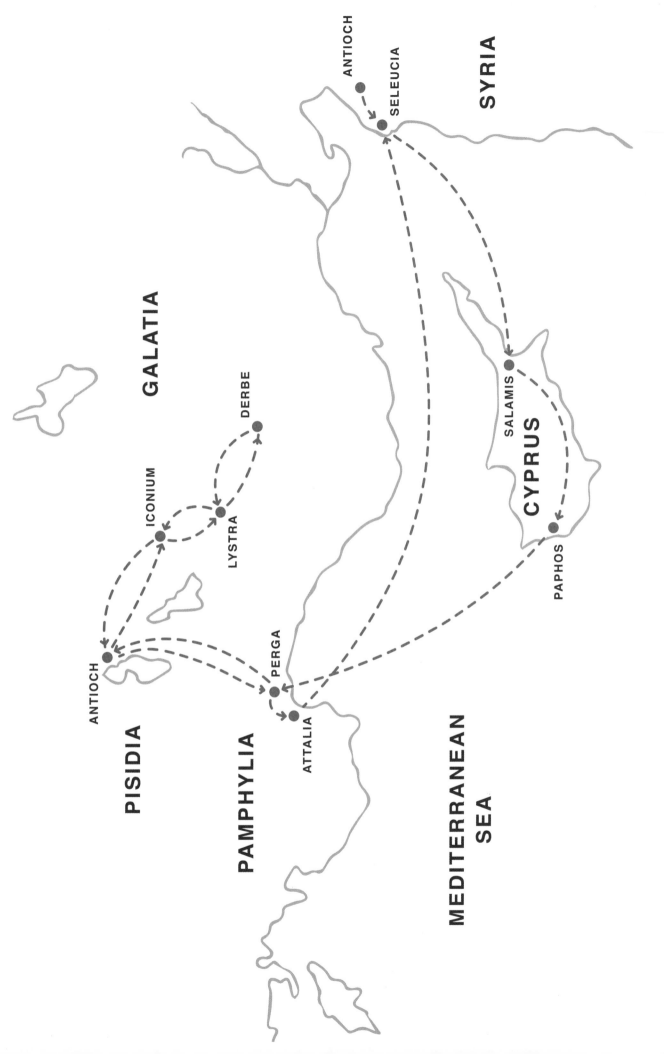

PAUL'S FIRST MISSIONARY JOURNEY

SYRIA

ANTIOCH

SELEUCIA

GALATIA

DERBE

ICONIUM

LYSTRA

CYPRUS

SALAMIS

PAPHOS

ANTIOCH

PERGA

PISIDIA

ATTALIA

PAMPHYLIA

MEDITERRANEAN SEA

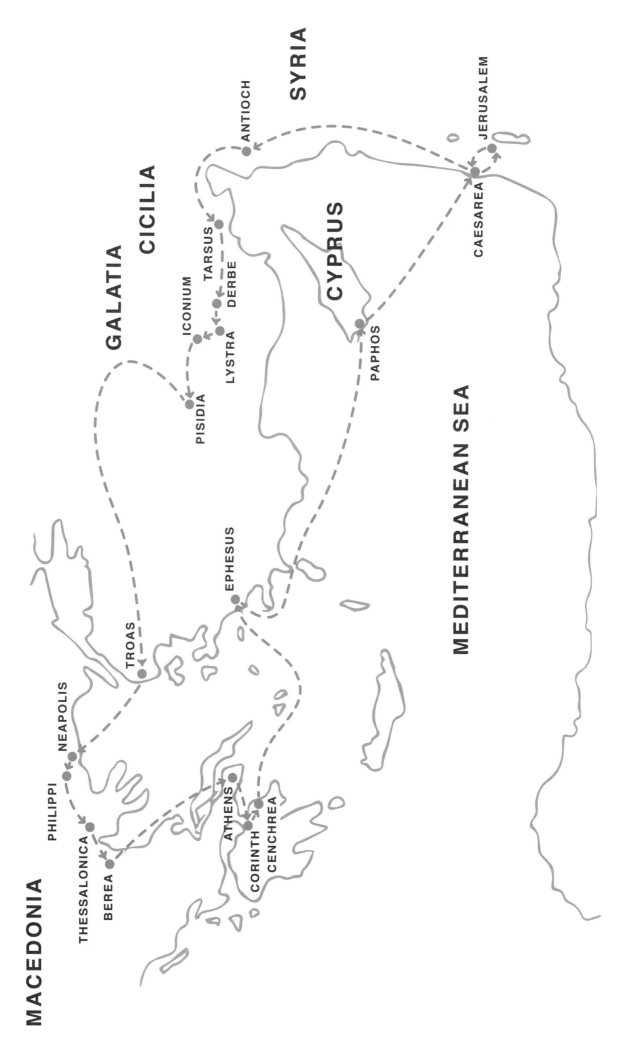

PAUL'S SECOND MISSIONARY JOURNEY

MACEDONIA

PHILIPPI
NEAPOLIS
THESSALONICA
BEREA
ATHENS
CORINTH
CENCHREA
TROAS
GALATIA
CICILIA
PISIDIA
ICONIUM
TARSUS
LYSTRA
DERBE
ANTIOCH
SYRIA
CYPRUS
PAPHOS
CAESAREA
JERUSALEM
EPHESUS
MEDITERRANEAN SEA

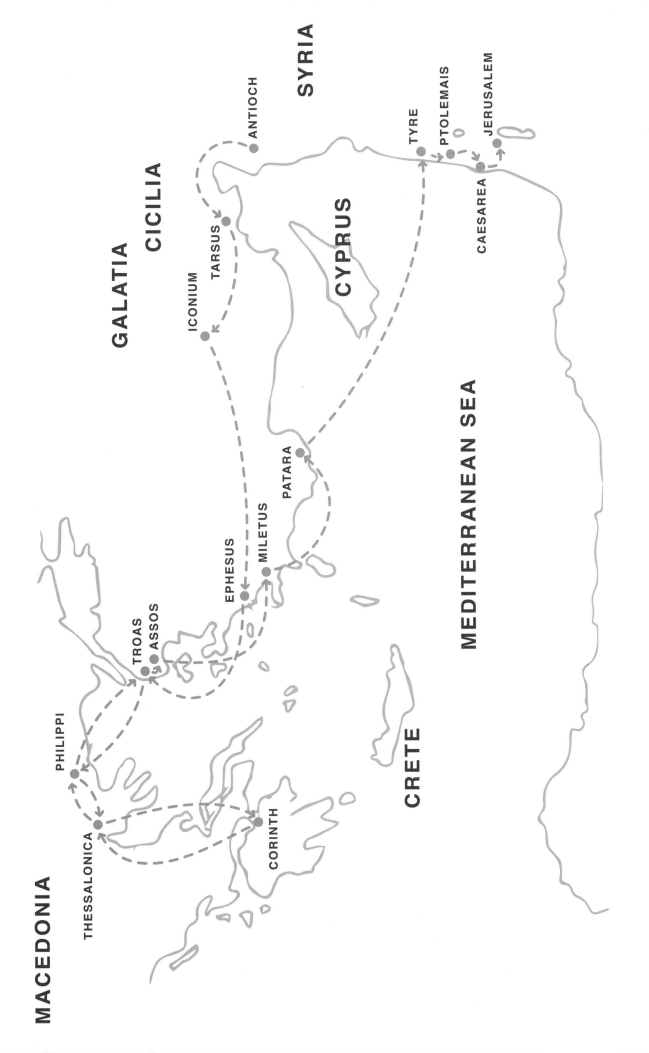

MATTHEW

AUTHOR

The author of the first Gospel in the New Testament was Matthew, a disciple and former tax collector.

DATE

Matthew wrote his Gospel around AD 50 to 55, most likely from Antioch.

AUDIENCE

The content of Matthew is heavily focused on Jesus being the Messiah, the King of the Jews, which means his audience was almost completely Jewish.

REASON

Matthew was written to show the Jewish people that Jesus was the Messiah they had been waiting for.

THEME

Jesus is the Jewish Messiah, the fullfullment of Old Testament prophecy.

KEY VERSE

"Do not think that I have come to abolish the Law or the Prophets; I have not come to abolish them but to fulfill them." (5:17 ESV)

SECTIONS

Ministry in Galilee (Ch 1-7), Miracles and Kingdom Parables (Ch 8-3), End of Galilean Ministry (Ch 14-18), Ministry in Perea and Judea (Ch 19-25), Passion, Death, and Resurrection (Ch 26-28)

KEY WORDS

Kingdom, Covenant, Fulfilled, Father, Spirit

THE BOOK

The Gospel of Matthew is the first book in the New Testament, which is important because Matthew is a Jew writing to the Jews and he shows them that their Messiah has arrived. It's a phenomenal book of fulfillment.

One thing to remember when looking at the four Gospels is to put yourself in the shoes of the original reader so that you can better understand what is being taught. In this case, Matthew uses far more Old Testament quotes than the other Gospel writers and doesn't feel obligated to explain the Jewish lifestyle. The audience would have understood all of that.

Right off the bat, Matthew records Jesus' genealogy through Mary, the bloodline/legal line of Jesus. He shows how Jesus was a descendant of David and Abraham, two of the most fundamental people in the Jewish faith, both of whom the Messiah was promised to come from. Genealogies may not be very important to us as Gentiles, but this genealogy alone has caused many Jews to come to faith in Christ. Genealogies mean everything. It's your DNA. It's what makes you, you.

What were the two covenants that God had with Abraham and David?
(Gen 15 and 2 Sam 7)

The five women in Jesus' genealogy are listed below. **Who were they?**

1. **Tamar** (Gen 38)

2. **Rahab** (Josh 2)

3. **Ruth** (Ruth)

4. **Bathsheba** (2 Sam 11-12)

5. **Mary** (Matt 1:18-25)

Notice how Matthew started off the story of Jesus at his baptism. An interesting thing to point out is that the Father, Son, and Holy Spirit were all present during it. Many believe that the Father, Son and Holy Spirit were also present at Creation, too. **What evidence do you find in Genesis 1 for that belief?**

Right after Jesus' baptism he was brought into the wilderness to be tempted by Satan for 40 days. The number 40 is often associated with testing and trials, which we saw in the Old Testament as the Israelites wandered in the wilderness for 40 years.

Can you think of other comparisons between those two situations that we should take note of?

Once John the Baptist completed his task of finalizing the Old Testament and ushering in the New, Jesus put a spin on the message of salvation and taught about kingdom principles. The word "kingdom" broken down means the "king's domain" and since it's the kingdom of heaven, Jesus was implying that God controls everything where the Kingdom is present.

When you meditate on the phrase "kingdom of heaven", what comes to mind?

Blessed are the poor in spirit, for theirs is the kingdom of heaven.

Blessed are those who mourn, for they will be comforted.

Blessed are the meek, for they will inherit the earth.

Blessed are those who hunger and thirst for righteousness, for they will be filled.

Blessed are the merciful, for they will be shown mercy.

Blessed are the pure in heart, for they will see God.

Blessed are the peacemakers, for they will be called children of God.

Blessed are those who are persecuted because of righteousness,

for theirs is the kingdom of heaven.

---

the beatitudes

Jesus said that he came to fulfill the Law, not abolish it. Matthew actually records the term "fulfilled" fifteen times in reference to Christ in his Gospel. Jesus also said that not one jot or tittle would pass from the Law before it was fulfilled. As we just saw while studying the Old Testament, there was a lot that has yet to be fulfilled.

So, what does that mean for us? What does that mean for the Jews?

It's amazing to see that Matthew was able to record all five of Jesus' main sermons word-for-word in this book. He had to have been ferociously jotting down notes every time that Jesus began a discourse or the Holy Spirit reminded him of Jesus' words.

What is the main focus of each of Jesus' five sermons?

1. **Matt 5-7**

2. **Matt 10**

3. **Matt 13**

4. **Matt 18**

5. **Matt 23-25**

How do they relate with each other?

Read Matthew 6:25-33. Jesus affirms the promise of provision among those that dedicate their life to Him. He promises to provide so we can hold Him accountable to that promise. The key to provision is seeking first the Kingdom and His righteousness. Then our needs will be met.

So often I hear people say that they wish they could do "Christian" work for a living. ALL WORK is Christian work. Every believer is in full-time ministry. We are all missionaries that have been charged with the task of making disciples in our surroundings. If you work at McDonald's, you are called to preach the gospel message to your peers. If you are the CEO of a Fortune 500 company, you are called to preach the gospel message to your peers. If you are living in a yurt in Africa and preaching the gospel message to your peers, you are called to continue preaching the gospel message to your peers. Once we have that realization and begin acting upon righteousness, God will provide for every one of our needs.

Have you ever witnessed God provide in a supernatural way? If so, what happened?

As we see in Chapter 13, Jesus loved speaking in parables to his audiences.

Why does Jesus speak in parables? (Matt 13:13-17)

When Matthew gets to the Mount of Transfiguration, we see Elijah and Moses talking to Jesus. That's interesting because Moses wasn't allowed into the Promised Land while he was still alive because his inheritance was knowing God. Now that he is in his glorified body, he was allowed in.

What do you think our glorified bodies will be like? Will our appearance be different? How old do you think we will be?

The last words of Jesus that Matthew records, are, "All authority in heaven and on earth has been given to me. Go therefore and make disciples of all nations, baptizing them in the name of the Father and of the Son and of the Holy Spirit, teaching them to observe all that I have commanded you. And behold, I am with you always, to the end of the age" (28:18b-20 ESV). That statement is what is known as the Great Commission.

In what ways are you fulfilling the Great Commission? How can you improve?

FINAL THOUGHTS

The Gospel of Matthew is all about Jesus. As a Jew. For the Jews. The climax of faith.

Matthew is a genius in his penmanship because he displays one prophecy after the next from the Old Testament, confirming that Jesus Christ is the one true Messiah that they had all been waiting for. From the location of his birth, to his means of transportation into Rome as the King - it IS all there and it HAS BEEN all there.

From the beginning, God promised a Messiah would come one day and save His people. Jesus is the one.

The sad fact is that many people missed it. They couldn't comprehend the fact that the Messiah had actually come because it all seemed too good to be true and he didn't present himself as a "Conquering King" like everyone expected. As we see time and time again, Yahweh is a God of second chances. He knows it's hard for us to accept things, especially something that brilliant, the first time around.

The good news is that he is coming back. He will come one day to reign supreme and judge every person accordingly.

After studying the Old Testament for the last nine months or so, what are some ways that you could show a Jewish person that Jesus is their Messiah?

AUTHOR

The Gospel of Mark was written by the man himself, Mark (Latin version) John Mark (Hebrew).

DATE

There is a lot of debate about which Gospel was written first. Some believe that Matthew and Luke were first, with Mark pulling his stories from them, while others believe that Mark wrote first and Matthew and Luke drew from him. We do not know for sure which one it is.

AUDIENCE

The Gospel of Mark was written to Christians in Rome. If Mark was written at a later date, we know that there were thousands of Christians being martyred in Rome at the time. We also know that the early church met down in the Catacombs, the graveyard of martyrs. They didn't do it to hide, but to remind themselves of the risk they were taking. That's where Mark would have read this Gospel to the other believers. Think about how much more impactful that would make the story.

REASON

Mark shows Jesus as a suffering servant in order to encourage the audience to press on through any form of persecution that they were dealing with. He shows the power and actions of Jesus more than the other gospels in order to prove this servant was truly the King.

THEME

Jesus as the suffering servant.

KEY VERSE

"For even the Son of Man did not come to be served, but to serve, and to give His life as a ransom for many." (10:45 ESV)

SECTIONS

Jesus' Ministry (Ch 1-10), Passion Week (Ch 11-16)

KEY WORDS/PHRASES

Immediately, Authority, Spirit, Kingdom of God

MARK

THE BOOK

Mark is a unique book, in that it highlights miracles far more than teachings. He includes 18 miracles in these 16 chapters, with only four parables and one major discourse. Mark does not give any of Christ's ancestry, since the theme is that Christ is a servant, and people don't care about a servant's ancestry.

None of the Gospels identify the author because they don't want the attention to be on themselves at all. Mark is in this same category.

Who was Mark?
Mark was too young to be a disciple, but he was fascinated with Jesus so he hung around him as much as possible. There is a chance that his house was used to host the disciples in the Upper Room. He was also most likely the naked guy that ran away in the Garden of Gethsemane when Jesus was arrested. Mark never had the spotlight on himself, but he did end up helping Barnabas and Paul on multiple journeys.

Mark himself was hyperactive. The word "immediately" is repeated 41x because he was always on the go from one place to the next. He couldn't sit still and wanted to be front and center in all of the action. That's why the book of Mark focuses so heavily on the actions of Jesus instead of his sermons.

Therefore, the first eight chapters are all about healings, miracles, and casting out demons. Which one of these stories is your favorite? Why?

In Chapter 5, Jesus and the disciples take a trip to the other side of the Sea of Galilee, into the country of the Gerasenes, and are met with a demoniac waiting for them on the shore. One thing to understand is that the Galilean side of the Sea of Galilee (on the left) was the Jewish, "clean" side. The Decapolis side (on the right) was the Gentile, "unclean" side. Seeing the legion on the Gentile side must have absolutely freaked them out because that's exactly what they expected the Gentile side to be like. Savages.

How did Jesus set the demoniac free? (Mk 5:6-13) **What does that teach us about demons?**

After setting the demoniac free, Jesus allowed him to be the first qualified preacher of the gospel, to other Gentiles. That's interesting.

In Chapters 6 and 8 we have the feeding of the 5,000 and 4,000. **Why do you think both were included? How much was left over at each?** (Mk 6:43, 8:8) **Do you see any significance in those numbers?**

After years of mentoring the disciples, Jesus is sitting with them at the base of Mt. Hermon in Caesarea Philippi. He asks them questions about himself to see if they truly believed that he was who he said he was. And the disciples passed the test. This was the first time that Jesus mentioned the Church, and the cross, the events of which were to happen shortly. It was at this point, when Peter said he believed Jesus was the Son of God, that Jesus was able to break the difficult news to them. God's plan of redemption was almost complete.

What did Peter do after Jesus foretold his death and resurrection? (Mk 8:32) **Why did Jesus say to Peter, "Get away from me, Satan?"** (Mk 8:33)

FISHERS OF MEN

Towards the end of the Gospel, Mark decided to narrow his focus and really display the reason for Christ's arrival in Jerusalem (and on earth in general). Mark gives us the most in-depth look at the final week than in all of the Gospels.

Jesus knew what was going to happen, and it wasn't pretty. His life was to be laid down as an exchange for all of the sins of humanity. He actually became sin so we could be seen as sinless. Every disease, every anger issue, every addiction, every evil desire from the past, present, and future were nailed to the cross so we could be set free. What we struggle with today was already taken care of 2,000 years ago. If Jesus is your personal Savior, you are FREE. Like, RIGHT NOW!

Have you had a revelation of that concept yet? How does that change the way you live?

In 15:38, Mark says that the Temple veil was torn from top to bottom. **What do you think that represented?**

Just as we saw when studying Zechariah, everything that Jesus said and did was a fulfillment of Old Testament prophecy. And it was fulfilled literally to a "T". That's why I believe it is so important for us to study and understand the Old Testament today. Jesus was a Jew that came to save the Jews first. How are we supposed to understand the importance of what he did/said if we don't understand the Jewish mindset? It's nearly impossible and we would miss out on SO much. That's why I am so pumped that you took the time to do the first part of this study to really dive into the OT!

FINAL THOUGHTS

As I said earlier, Mark was writing this Gospel to Roman Christians, many of whom were Gentiles. This Gospel is a great starting point for unbelievers or new believers because it is written to allow Gentiles to understand it. It's the basics. It shows what Jesus did and what we are called to do. I would encourage you to use this book for evangelism purposes.

With that said, put together a quick and simple "plan of evangelism", based on this Gospel. Cover the main points of Jesus' life, the importance of the cross, and how we are to respond.

Remember: Your audience won't have any understanding of the Old Testament, so give an overview in the most easy-to-understand way possible.

AUTHOR

The Gospel of Luke was written by a friend of Paul's, named Luke. Two important things to note while studying this book as well as the book of Acts is that Luke was a doctor and also a Gentile.

DATE

This Gospel was most likely written while Paul was imprisoned in Caesarea around AD 58-60 or during his Roman imprisonment in AD 60-62.

AUDIENCE

Luke addressed his Gospel to one man only: "most excellent Theophilus." So, who in the world is Theophilus?

Scholars have made many different claims over the years as to who Theophilus actually was. Some say that he was Paul's financial supporter, some believe he was Luke's master, while others believe that he was the Roman official or judge during Paul's trial.

I choose to agree with the last of the three main options. Luke does an amazing job at compiling all of his information from eye witness interviews and then presents the case that neither Jesus nor Paul had any big issues with the Roman government. Also, Luke ends the Book of Acts just before Paul's hearing...the same time when these writings would be presented to the judge.

REASON

As we just saw, this entire Gospel was written to support Paul in order to be set free and continue his journey of bringing the gospel around the world. It is an amazing look at the gospel story from the perspective of a Gentile doctor who focused on the humanity of the Son of Man.

THEME

Christ is the Savior for the Gentiles, too.

KEY VERSE

"For the Son of Man came to seek and save the lost." (19:10 ESV)

SECTIONS

The Incarnation (Ch 1-3), The Galilean Ministry (Ch 4-9), Journey Toward Jerusalem (Ch 10-19), Final Week (Ch 19-24)

KEY WORDS/PHRASES

Son of Man, Salvation, Kingdom, Pray

When studying the four Gospels, the most important thing that you can do is look at the stories through the eyes of the writer. In this case, as we saw earlier, Luke is writing to a Roman judge on behalf of his buddy Paul. Therefore, the content is much more focused on how Jesus interacted with Gentiles, Romans, and women…all of which hit home for Jesus.

Luke is a very unique book in the sense that it has many stories that the other authors did not have because they weren't able to interview the right people. Remember, this is being used as a court document and Luke was not present during the ministry of Jesus so he had to get information from all of the eyewitnesses that he could, in order to piece together the proper angle for Paul's pending release. That's why the feel of this book seems a little different compared to the other Gospels.

Luke, being a doctor, approached Jesus from the perspective of the Son of Man. Hence the reason for Jesus' genealogy dating back to the first man, Adam, through the line of Mary.

How do the other Gospels show Jesus' genealogy?

Matthew:

Mark:

John:

Luke found it important to spend a lot of time looking at the different healing miracles of Jesus' ministry, not specifically to show the Romans that Jesus was God, but because, as a doctor, he was fascinated with them himself. The recordings are truly unbelievable to those that have not experienced or witnessed the power of God. Luke, also loves looking at the Holy Spirit more than the other writers because of the power that He produces through the natural man. That's why Luke and the book of Acts are more focused on being baptized in the Spirit and the workings of Jesus' disciples.

Of all of the stories that are unique to Luke, which one speaks to you the most? Why?

At the beginning of Luke, we get this great story of Mary, who was pregnant with Jesus, visiting Elizabeth, who was pregnant with John the Baptist at the time. When Mary greeted Elizabeth, John leaped in her womb because the presence of God was so strong upon her and her spoken word changed something in the atmosphere.

John the Baptist seemed to acknowledge a change in the spiritual realm even though he was not even born yet.

How does this story affect your views on abortion?

What does this show about children's discernment of the spiritual realm? How should this influence the way that we raise our children?

Luke is also the only Gospel that records anything about Jesus' life before his actual ministry began. We see this wild story of him being left in Jerusalem after his bar mitzvah at the age of 12. How could his parents have left him behind?! He was God in the flesh!

Why do you think the Holy Spirit made sure that this story was included in the text?

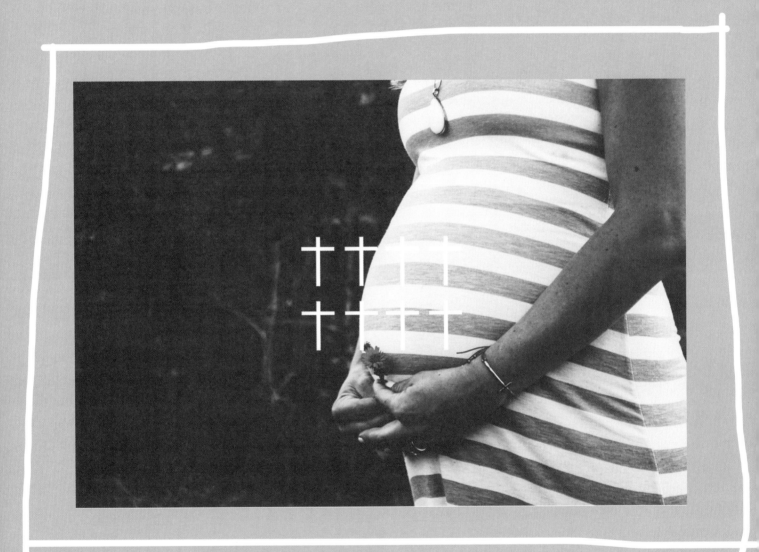

What do you think Jesus meant when he said, "didn't you know I had to be in my Father's house" (2:49 NIV)**?** Remember that he had not yet received the Holy Spirit, and this was around 18 years before his ministry began.

Luke ended up spending a lot of time focusing on women…showing how they were loved and cherished by Jesus far more than the religious leaders ever were. Yet sometimes in the church today, we can discount women in ministry and exalt the male religious leaders instead…Doesn't that seem to be the opposite of what Jesus taught? Remember, everything that Jesus did, he saw his Father doing first. I may be ruffling a few feathers here, but conviction isn't taken lightly most of the time.

How can we better serve the women of our communities today?

The Gospel of Luke is really written for everybody, Jew and Gentile alike. Luke was a Gentile writing to a Gentile so this Gospel should be used as an evangelism tool towards Gentiles. It's what the Holy Spirit had in mind from the beginning.

Which other Gospel can be used for evangelism to Gentiles?

Let's take a trip back to an important book in the Old Testament called Exodus. As we saw when studying that book, God conducted many miracles through the life of Moses in front of the eyes of Pharaoh. The final plague that was placed upon them was the death of the firstborn in every household. But the Jews were given a way out of it. They were required to sprinkle the blood of a lamb over their doorpost at night, and the angel of death would pass over their house, hence the name Passover.

After reading about the death of Jesus and also remembering the Passover in Exodus, list things that show Jesus was the fulfillment of Passover:

This book is only the start of Luke's collection of the stories. The book of Acts, also written by Luke, will show us how good of a Father we serve and the power that is meant to accompany the life of every believer.

FINAL THOUGHTS

Luke really is a Gospel for everybody. He includes many important testimonies that we don't read about in the other Gospels. And all of these are used to teach us new things.

Testimonies are among the greatest things that we could ever share with the world. They produce hunger. They produce connection. They can also boost faith in hopes that God will work for us in the same way that He has for others.

Sharing our life stories and what Jesus means to us are the least we can do for those we love. With that said, this week your task is to write a blog post that looks at what the perfect sacrifice of Jesus means to you and the way that you live out your faith. If you feel compelled, please share your post with others on any form of social media or through email. Have fun with it!

SEEK

SAVE

AUTHOR

The Gospel of John was written by the apostle John himself. He was the only disciple still alive, and times were changing before his eyes.

DATE

John wrote his Gospel sometime in the AD 80's before the persecution of Domitian began. This was his first book with four or more to come before his death in AD 98.

AUDIENCE

The Gospel of John was written to various churches around Asia Minor where he had an influence. John was one of the elders in the church of Ephesus and was looked up to because of his experiences and wisdom.

REASON

John was written to show the audience that Jesus was both fully God and fully man. It was most likely used to provide information that the other Gospels left out and to show more of a theological perspective on the life of Christ.

THEME

Jesus came to give eternal life because he is God.

KEY VERSE

"I came that they may have life and have it abundantly." (10:10b ESV)

SECTIONS

Ministry and Rejection (Ch 1-11), Passion Week and Resurrection (Ch 12-21)

KEY WORDS

Believe, Heaven, Father, Eternal

THE BOOK

The Gospel of John is 90% unique from the Synoptic Gospels as he explores Jesus from the Son of God perspective, including his preexistent genealogy at the beginning of his writing. Whereas the other Gospels looked at what Jesus did and said, John approaches his story from the inside by looking at how Jesus felt and who he was as a person. He made it a point to show that Jesus is fully human and fully divine at the same time. There was nothing that Jesus could do while on Earth without help from the Father.

In John 15:5 Jesus says something similar regarding us. What is it?

John had decades to map out his version of the Gospel message since he lived longer than any other disciple. He decided to write his Gospel nearly 30 years later than the others. He didn't want people wasting their time figuring out who Jesus was so he put it all out on the table.

Isn't it amazing that the Creator of the universe came down to his creation just to save it? **Describe a time when you worked extra hard on a project and it didn't turn out as you planned. How did that make you feel? How do you think God felt?**

In Chapter 1, we are introduced to a man named John the Baptist (not to be confused with the author) who was the forerunner to the Messiah and the Old Testament closes with a preview of John in Malachi 4:5.

Who was "the Lamb of God" that John baptized? What do you think was the reason for his baptism?

What happened during Jesus' baptism that caused John to realize who he was?

Back in the day, Jews would study the Torah over their entire childhood in hopes of one day being selected by a Rabbi to train and eventually be a Rabbi themselves. At their bar mitzvah, a Rabbi would come up to them and say, "follow me". From that moment forward, the trainee would mimic every move and word of the Rabbi so that they would be a direct representation of their Rabbi. Since all of the disciples were working in their family occupation when Jesus found them, it meant that they had all been turned down by the local Rabbis. Jesus gave them a chance. Those two words, "follow me", were worth dropping everything in order to follow.

Would you have dropped everything if you hadn't known who Jesus was?

How do you think their family members felt? What would you do if your son just ran off to follow the new Rabbi in town?

One thing to notice in all of John's books is that he writes in sevens. Seven is the number of perfect divinity and is a very important number in the Jewish faith. The top two things that John focuses on in this Gospel are seven major miracles as well as seven "I AM" statements.

List the seven miracles that he points out:

1. John 2:1-11

2. John 4:43-54

3. **John 5:1-9**

Water to wine seems like a strange one to start with, doesn't it? He performed this one privately to the disciples so that they could see the power that was at hand, showing that he truly was the Lord. To run out of wine at a wedding was a major faux-pas so Jesus freed them of their embarrassment and even cranked the party up another level. He was more concerned with bringing joy to the lives of others than what was to come for his future.

4. **John 6:1-14**

5. **John 6:16-21**

What role does joy play in your day-to-day faith? Where does joy come from? (Gal 5:22-23) How can you increase it?

6. **John 9:1-33**

7. **John 11:1-44**

What do you think the most popular verse in the Bible is? John 3:16? Notice how it is spoken to one man at night. There is no stage or microphone. It's one on one. Just the way God likes it.

What do all of these miracles show you about Jesus?

Why do you think God chose to do it this way instead of preaching it from a mountain top?

The first miracle that Jesus performs in this Gospel is to turn water into wine, but before doing so, he stated that his "hour has not yet come", which meant that he was not ready to die yet. The beginning of his ministry marked the countdown to his death.

Then the woman at the well story comes up, and people are shocked by Jesus' actions. They couldn't believe that he was talking to a Samaritan woman. The Samaritans were considered half-breed sell-outs because their distant relatives intermingled with Gentiles from Samaria after returning from exile, even though they were commanded not to do so. Not only was this woman a Samaritan, but the fact that she was a woman in general would not have made sense for a Jewish man to talk to her in broad daylight. Jesus didn't care about societal norms. He showed her love from the bottom of his heart because he knew her worth.

Who does society tell you that you "shouldn't talk to"? What can you do to show them their worth?

In Chapter 6, John shares with us the first of seven "I AM" statements. Those statements meant everything to John.

List all seven of them below:

1. **John 6:35**

2. **John 8:12**

3. **John 10:9**

4. **John 10:11**

5. **John 11:25**

6. **John 14:6**

7. **John 15:5**

I AM.

Jesus calls himself the "good shepherd" in Chapter 10, and states that his sheep know his voice. If you know anything about sheep, you know that they are dumb, defenseless, and easily frightened. Pet sheep on the other hand, because they are loved, are actually super smart, can live up to their full potential, and they have no fear.

Write a prayer about being more aware of your need for Jesus as a Shepherd:

As Jesus was entering Jerusalem on a donkey, the people placed palm branches on the road before him as an act of honoring a King. Despite all of Jesus' teaching, they still expected Jesus to be the political Messiah that was talked about so often by the Prophets. They just didn't realize then that there would be two comings. They wanted Jesus to establish his worldly kingdom then and now. Think of how confused they must have been when he headed straight for the temple instead of the throne…

The good news for us is that his Kingdom does reign in the hearts of His children right now and can impact the world around us if we allow it to. Jesus told his disciples to pray for heaven to come to earth and we should be focusing on the same every day.

What do you think it looks like to bring heaven to earth every day?

The day that Jesus rose from the dead was the most joyous day in the history of the world. It changed EVERYTHING! It's interesting to note that Mary doesn't recognize Jesus right away, but knows it is him when he says her name. Remember, "my sheep hear my voice… and they follow me" (John 10:27 NASB).

Why do you think Mary didn't recognize Jesus? Do you think he had a different appearance?

At the end of this Gospel, Jesus questioned Simon Peter three times as to whether or not he loves him. Earlier, Peter had denied that he knew Jesus three times. This was the cancelling out of these denials. By looking at Peter's letters in the New Testament we know that he ended well and continued loving Christ for the rest of his life.

FINAL THOUGHTS

John focused heavily on the fact that Jesus was fully God and fully man at the same time. What amazing news for all of us!

How does that understanding impact your view of Jesus? What does that mean for your own faith journey?

When others deny Jesus' deity or humanity, what verses could you share with them from John's Gospel? (see John 1:1 for starters)

HAVE
LIFE
AND
LIFE
ABUNDANTLY

AUTHOR

As with the Gospel of Luke, the book of Acts was also written by Dr. Luke, a friend of Paul's. Luke shows that they were together during many of the travels and experienced the same miracles throughout.

DATE

Whereas the Gospel of Luke was written during Paul's Caesarean or Roman imprisonment, this book was written shortly after, during his imprisonment between AD 60 to 62.

AUDIENCE

Along with the Gospel of Luke, this book is also addressed to "Most Excellent Theophilus."

Considering that Luke ends this book with Paul still awaiting trial, it seems as if the evidence for this being used as a document in the trial is increasing. Therefore, Theophilus might have been a Roman judge at the time.

REASON

The book of Acts was used as a legal document to serve as a testimony on behalf of Paul's missionary journeys. Thank goodness that we still have it today because this book is a great historical account of the early Christian church.

THEME

The gospel message is for everyone, everywhere.

KEY VERSE

"But you will recieve power when the Holy Spirit has come upon you; and you will be my witness in Jerusalem, and all Judea and Samaria, and to the end of the earth." (1:8 ESV)

SECTION

To the Jews and Samaritans (Ch 1-8), To the Rest of the World (Ch 9-28)

KEY WORDS

Believe, Holy Spirit, Baptized, Witness, Church

THE BOOK

The book of Acts is a historical look at the first 30 years of the early church and, in many cases, could be used as a model for missionary work around the world today.

The book starts off with Jesus promising the disciples that they would receive the power of the Holy Spirit shortly and would end up preaching in Jerusalem, Judea and Samaria, and to the remotest parts of the earth. Each one of those places is another ring outside of their current sphere of influence. It can be used as a great plan for evangelism today no matter where you are located.

What is your church's mission statement for missions?

After instructing the disciples regarding the Holy Spirit, Jesus ascended into heaven and left them with a hope to hold onto.

Considering the betrayal and death of Judas Iscariot, the disciples were now reduced to a group of eleven men. A meeting was held in the Upper Room with 120 other Jews, in order to cast lots for Judas' replacement. Matthias was the selected candidate, and the new twelfth apostle.

In Chapter 2, an amazing thing took place among them. They were all filled with the Holy Spirit again and everyone began to speak in different tongues. So much so that people called them out as being drunk.

Some believe in a baptism of the Holy Spirit, which is different from an initial receiving of the Holy Spirit, while others believe in water baptism only.

Peter says in 2:38, "Repent, and each of you be baptized in the name of Jesus Christ for the forgiveness of your sins; and you will receive the gift of the Holy Spirit" (NASB).

Have you been water baptized? When? If not, have you thought about it?

Do you remember what happened at the first Pentecost in the Old Testament? (Exodus 32:25-29)

Fast forward almost 1,500 years and in Acts 2:41 Luke shows us that on this Day of Pentecost, 3,000 souls were saved. Whereas the Law brought death to 3,000 people; the Holy Spirit brought life. It's an amazing illustration of God's sovereignty.

After this life-changing experience, the Church was finally able to begin building itself up based on what they had been taught through Jesus' ministry. It was go-time.

It's safe to say that they were hit with quite a bit of resistance right off the bat. That seems to be the case any time the Holy Spirit moves in mighty ways, even today.

Skepticism is one of the Church's biggest threats. Much of the Church has distanced itself so far from accepting any sign or wonder as being from God that it looks at them as fake or even demonic. Sounds like what Jesus was dealing with, with the religious leaders, doesn't it?

I too was very skeptical. Then I began to witness the Holy Spirit move.

One morning at the beginning of my stint in Australia we were having a time of worship before getting the day started. Being that I grew up in a pretty conservative church I felt like a fish out of water standing next to people that were lifting their hands and even dancing. Then to really top it off, one of the leaders went up front to the microphone and asked if there was an interpreter in the room because God had given him a tongue to share. "A what?!", I thought.

An interpreter raised her hand.
The leader opened his mouth.

Man, I was freaked out because the power of the Holy Spirit was never even taught about in the church that I grew up in, let alone someone speaking in what seemed to be gibberish. Next thing I knew, the entire atmosphere of the room shifted as the presence of God broke various strongholds on people's lives and gave them freedom that only He can bring. I had no idea if I should believe what I was seeing/feeling or not. But I knew that if this was truly from God then I wanted all of it.

Have you ever experienced the Holy Spirit moving around you? If so, what happened?

What do you think was going through Ananias' mind when the Lord told him to heal Saul, the man who was persecuting all of his friends?

Moving on, Stephen was a man that wouldn't let anybody sway him from his understanding of the truth. He met with the Sanhedrin so that he could explain what was happening to all of these Jews that were now following "The Way". His discourse is the entire gospel message that came out of the failures of Israel's past. The Sanhedrin wouldn't have any of what he was saying though and that stoning sparked the persecution of Christians throughout Jerusalem and was being led by a man named Saul.

Saul was a bad dude. He was a Jewish Roman citizen who studied under Gamaliel, the top of the top for rabbis. Saul was so hardcore in his faith that he made it a point to throw anyone in prison that went against his beliefs, especially this new group of Christians.

When Saul was on the road to Damascus with hopes of throwing more Christians in prison, he was stopped by Jesus himself and ended up being blinded until a man named Ananias comes to heal him of it. Saul was converted on the spot and asks Ananias to baptize him.

We know that Saul went to his hometown of Tarsus for ten years in order to preach there and build himself up, before going out on any missionary journeys.

What about us? Do our hometowns see the fire in each of us? They need to see our changed life before the world will. How can you use Saul as an example regarding hometown missionary work instead of just doing short-term mission trips every once in a while?

Many people in the Church talk about having a Saul-Paul conversion once they became saved, but that just isn't biblical at all. Once Saul is converted, his name remains Saul. It isn't until he begins his first missionary journey to the Gentiles that he switches over to his Roman name of Paul. It's only fitting since he claimed to become all things to all people, and if he was preaching to Roman citizens it would make sense for him to use his Roman name.

If you flip back to the New Testament Overview, there are maps that show the routes of Paul's travels, and you can follow along as you go back through the book.

His first journey included the cities of Salamis, Paphos, Antioch, Iconium, Lystra and Derbe.

Do you think Paul dealt with any fear of what others thought of him during his first time out? How do you think he overcame that fear?

In Chapter 15, we have the infamous Jerusalem Council.

What was the council debating? What was the final consensus? What does that mean for us?

Paul departed on his second missionary journey, this time traveling to the cities Philippi, Thessalonica, Berea, Athens, Corinth, and Ephesus. Many cities in which Paul wrote letters to later on in the New Testament.

During this journey, Paul ended his travels with Barnabas, because he didn't want to preach alongside John Mark anymore. So Barnabas takes John Mark in one direction, and Paul goes the other way with Silas and eventually Timothy.

ADVENTURE IS CALLING

Paul becomes very close with Timothy and eventually has him circumcised. **What do you think was the reason for his circumcision if Paul spoke so strongly against it at the Jerusalem Council?**

Paul tried to travel to Bithynia, but the Holy Spirit had different plans for him. Luke writes that the "the spirit of Jesus would not allow them to" (16:7 NIV).

Have you ever been blocked by the Holy Spirit from going somewhere? If so, what happened?

Paul and the others ended up being directed through a vision to go over to Macedonia in Greece. Notice that Luke now includes "we" in his writing so this is where he joined the group to finish off the second journey. Once they arrived, Paul preached a very popular sermon on top of Mars Hill to all of the Macedonians. In his teaching, he uses a lot of Gentile jargon and cultural examples in order for them to understand what he was talking about. Modern day evangelism could take some notes on that one. It's incredibly important to meet people where they are at and be able to understand, instead of just preaching from a place of "perfection". We are all in this thing called life together.

Paul's third missionary journey was a pretty long one that ended up in Jerusalem. He spent extra time in some of the cities because the response in them was so great. An important thing to look at is that all of the disciples were out creating more disciples in each city. They didn't ask people to raise their hands and make a "decision", like today. They taught new believers from the ground-up and nurtured their faith alongside them.

Have you ever been mentored or discipled? Are you currently discipling anyone? How can you use this story as an example for evangelism?

In Chapters 23-26 we see the beginning of Paul's trial. It is the reason why this book was written in the first place. It's Rome vs. Christianity. Paul never harmed anybody on his journeys, he only healed them. So the guards were fairly lenient as they watched over him.

Even on the ship heading to Rome, the crew seemed to listen to Paul's prophecies and wisdom as a higher authority than their own common sense. We saw the same thing happen in the book of Jonah, if you remember.

They all eventually made it to Rome and Paul was placed on house arrest. He was still able to welcome visitors at any time though, and continued to preach the gospel message every day. That's where he sat writing letters to the churches which he had built on his journeys while awaiting the trial that was soon to take place. Considering that Paul was released in AD 62 and was able to depart on his fourth missionary journey from Rome, we can surmise that this letter was a successful witness regarding his life and ministry.

FINAL THOUGHTS

If you look at Acts from a personal perspective, it can be a very heavy book because much of the modern day church conducts itself far differently. Signs and wonders being used for evangelism purposes tend to only be for the "crazies" in the eyes of many, but in the Bible they always accompanied the preaching of the gospel. The disciples would FIRST show the power of God and THEN give them the Good News. They shared an experience of the Holy Spirit's presence FIRST because they knew that affecting hearts was far more life-changing than affecting heads. You can tell someone all day about why they should believe the Bible, but it may save you a lot of time and be more impactful if you just show them instead.

What are your thoughts on using signs and wonders for evangelism purposes?

ROMANS

AUTHOR

The book of Romans was written by the apostle Paul.

DATE

Romans was written on Paul's third missionary journey around AD 55 to 56. We know that he had not actually been to Rome yet and due to the similarities of 1+2 Corinthians, we can conclude that it was written in that timeframe.

AUDIENCE

Like I said, Paul was writing to a church that he had never visited before and/or known the leaders in Rome...we can conclude that from the entire chapter he used as a closing statement, to show that he knew the same people they did which would help build credibility with them. There was a ton of tension in the Roman church between Jews and Gentiles at the time, both making claims that they were in charge and and things would be done their way. Talk about a mess.

REASON

Romans was written to help resolve the tension between the Jews and Gentiles in Rome and to show that both groups were equal in God's sight. It was also written to explain the gospel as a whole, in order to be used for ministry advancement.

THEME

Basics of Christianity and Jew/Gentile relations.

KEY VERSE

"For I am not ashamed of the gospel for it is the power of God for salvation for everyone who believes; to the Jew first and also to the Greek. For in it the righteousness of God is revealed from faith for faith, as it is written; 'The righteous shall live by faith." (1:16-17 ESV)

SECTIONS

Paul's Gospel (Ch 1-8), The Gospel and Israel (Ch 9-11), Living the Gospel Out (Ch 12-16)

KEY WORDS

Law, Righteous, Grace, Justified, Faith, Gospel

THE BOOK

Romans is a massive book. There is a ton of deep content here that would take months to really dive into. That's why we are doing an overview of each book for now with the hope that you will take time in the future to go deeper, once you have a better understanding of the Bible as a whole.

Romans is the gospel. It's a book about grace and it's a book about redemption. This is God's plan for humanity. Therefore, it is extremely important that you take time to really understand this book.

Do you know what the word gospel means? If so, what?

Considering Paul was one of the most influential Jews at the time, he still maintained a Jewish mindset, even when reaching out to the Gentiles. Therefore, he understood his faith through the lens of a covenant relationship because that is what the Old Testament is heavily based on. So we must understand covenants too, in order to get what Paul is talking about.

Do you remember how a blood covenant is cut? I'll give you a little help:

The Kill:
The two people going into the covenant relationship began by finding a pure animal to sacrifice for the covenant ceremony. Once the animal had been selected, the two of them cut it in half along the spine, separating it to two sides. Remember, they didn't have saws back then like we have today so at this point they were covered in blood, sweat, and most likely tears. Completely. Exhausted.

The Oath:

After laying out both sides of the animal as a representation of the two parties involved, they would walk in a figure-8 throughout the halves, repeating the terms of the covenant as they did so.

Blood Brothers:

After the terms were stated multiple times, they would take a rock and cut a large slice on their right hand followed by putting their hands together. As we saw in Leviticus, blood means life. So their blood joining together symbolized their lives joining as well. Two became one. Then they would rub dirt in their wound in order to create a scar as a visible reminder of the covenant.

Party Time:

After all of the rituals were complete, the witnesses from each side of the covenant had a large party together. And those in attendance would become responsible for holding them accountable for their actions.

To enter into a covenant was a major deal. It meant that you died to yourself and there was no way out of it. Everything that you did revolved around the terms of the covenant.

What are the four main covenants of the Old Testament?

1. **Genesis 8**

2. **Genesis 15**

3. **Genesis 17**

4. **2 Samuel 7**

When God entered into a covenant with Abraham (Gen 15), He put him to sleep during the process and completed the figure-8 Himself employing fire and smoke. The reason that Abraham couldn't do the task was because he was still sinful, and God needed someone sinless to join Him. So, God basically made a down payment in order to show that the covenant was unconditional and eternal.

Two thousand years later we see that Jesus was the One without sin. Through him we enter into that covenant when we are washed clean by his blood. When we come to Jesus we are saying that we want to join in as a representative on his side of the covenant. We want to be a part of that covenant party now that it is complete. His representation allows us to be included in this whole thing. How amazing is that?!

The Bible is one big covenant being fulfilled/renewed. It isn't an old and a new one. It's the same covenant throughout.

Since we are under this covenant, God sees Jesus when He looks at each of us. That is our new identity. The two became one. The old has been forgotten, and we have been made completely new from the inside out. Being one with him means that we now have the same authority on earth as he did. We are his representatives here and now, spread out across the earth.

Jesus taught us to pray, "Your Kingdom come, your will be done, on earth as it is in Heaven" (Matthew 6:10 ESV) because He wants to see Heaven on earth NOW. We need to stop worrying about getting there and focus more on bringing it here. The covenant that we have accepted as our own allows us to do just that. By saying we agree with the covenant means we are charged with a task. Our new identity has expectations associated with it.

What do you think some of those expectations are?

Moving on to Chapter 5, why did God give the Law to Moses (5:20-21)**?**

For sin to increase? That's the opposite of our thinking, but the Law helped eliminate the possibility of man being able to justify his sinful nature.

The Law was also given to expose our sin nature in general, to show that we can't do it on our own, and to make us dependent on God at all times.

Since we are no longer under the Law, what exposes our sinfulness now? (John 16:8)

Remember we saw before that the Jews and Gentiles were fighting over who was in charge? Now Paul showed them that they were all sinners and he also showed them the three stages of salvation: justification, sanctification, and glorification.

What is justification? (It's ok to look these words up online if you don't know the definitions!)

HERE&NOW
HERE&NOW
HERE&NOW
HERE&NOW

What is sanctification?

What is glorification?

Justification, sanctification, and glorification are the three stages of salvation that Paul looks at in Chapters 5-8, but we must go back to see what other content he covered.

Romans 6:12 says, "Do not let sin continue to reign". **As good as that may sound, do you know how we can obey that command?**

Our sin was nailed to the cross and has no power over us. When we understand that, we can believe what God says about our process of salvation to actually be true. The justification and sanctification are true. You are truly a new creation all together. Satan legally has no dominion over you anymore. But you have the choice to believe what you want. You choose who you obey throughout the day. God never forces us to do or say anything. One of the biggest lies of the enemy is that we haven't been

changed…and, unfortunately, many times we believe it and act accordingly!

What have you accepted as truth about your identity, as a child of God, when you know it's really from Satan?

We are dead to our sin nature and have been given a new nature with a new identity. Being dead to sin means that we are free. It is not a battle going on inside of us like so many people teach. Yes, there is a battle going on outside that we are fighting, but it no longer has control of us. It's no longer a part of our identity. Now that we are new on the inside, we must learn how to live by the Spirit.

For some of you this is probably an entirely new concept, but it's exactly what God says about us. So if you truly believe in Him, you need to believe what He says. And he says that you are a new creation, wiped clean. When you go from the mindset of being a sinner to a saint and understand the fact that you are dead to sin, the negative influence that used to control your life will be turned to a positive one. And you will be set free to be far more joyful.

Is this all new content to you? If so, how does it make you feel?

Chapters 9-11 are fairly controversial because of what Paul says regarding physical Israel and the Jewish people. **What are your views on those chapters after studying the Old Testament as well as Romans?**

Paul gives a great illustration of what happens between Jews and Gentiles. Israel is shown as an olive tree in which branches that do not bear fruit are broken off and Gentile branches that do bear fruit are grafted in. So we, as believers in Jesus, have been brought into God's plan of redemption that began with the Hebrews and will end with the Hebrews.

In Chapter 12, Paul shows that we have everything we need right now in order to bring the Kingdom to earth, we just need to act on it.

We can sincerely love others and encourage them.
We can hate what is evil and love what is good.
We can bring peace to those who are suffering by introducing them to Jesus.

What other things would you add to the list?

The New Testament teaches us that we are supposed to be everything that Jesus was as a man. We are in covenant with God, so all of those things are now a part of our nature. If we don't walk them out, then we are acting against our nature. Jesus was fully God AND fully man, which means that he had to make the same moment-by-moment decisions that we do. That should give us confidence! We can do this!

In what ways would you like to be more like Jesus?

As I said earlier, and as you now know, Romans is a MASSIVE book. There is so much important information here that we need to spend time wrestling through. It is my prayer that you take time to continue studying this book at a later date and that God gives you a revelation of your new identity. As a believer in Jesus, you are now a saint. Sin has been rendered powerless because of what Jesus did for you…and me!

FINAL THOUGHTS

Looking at the Church as a whole today, I think you'll agree that we are divided… not walking in the unity Jesus desired for us. And often times we don't even try to understand those we disagree with.

One of the biggest divisions is between those who believe in the outworking of the Holy Spirit through signs and those that are just focused on head knowledge or learning the Bible.

Two different takes on Scripture. Tons of disagreements.

It all reminds me of the Jew and Gentile tension that Paul was dealing with when writing to the Romans. His main objective, besides preaching the gospel, was to unify the church. Each group had different views, but each group was necessary for the church to function properly.

Just like it is today. We get so caught up in which view is correct, when in reality Jesus is coming back for his Bride. Singular. Not his Non-Denominational Bride. Not his Pentecostal Bride. Not his Lutheran Bride. He is coming back for his ONE, spotless Bride.

We are all in this together. Jesus is coming back for US, the Church, and he loves his Bride more than anything.

So, as one group of people are being used by God to perform miracles and are speaking in tongues and another group is spending their time combing Scripture for answers on End Times theology, we need to love them the same.

Spirit and Scripture. Both are necessary.

How can you apply that understanding to your life today?

CORINTHIANS

AUTHOR

The author of both letters to the Corinthians was the apostle Paul.

DATE

First Corinthians was written between AD 55 and 56, while Paul was in Ephesus. Second Corinthians was written less than a year later from Philippi.

AUDIENCE

These two letters were written to the church in Corinth and were later shared among other churches in the area. Corinth was a major party city in it's time. We would compare it to Vegas today. It was a place of pleasure and indulgence. The Corinthians focus was self satisfaction. They weren't an easy bunch to deal with, but Paul was just the right guy for the job.

REASON

Paul was writing in order to help with church affairs based on reports from his friend Chloe's people and a letter sent by a group of Corinthians.

THEME

Love is the reason for everything.

KEY VERSE

"Let all that you do be done in love." (16:14 ESV)

SECTION

Reports from Chloe's People (Ch 1-6), Questions from the Corinthian's Letter (Ch 7-16)

KEY WORDS

Spirit, Body, Love, Church

FIRST LETTER

From what we can gather in these two letters, we learn that Paul had actually written four letters to the church of Corinth…two of which we have, two of which were lost.

The first problem that Paul addressed was the fact that the church was divided. People disagreed on who they liked best, what leader they preferred, who they were baptized by, etc. Those divisions are very similar to the divisions that we see in the church today.

In America, there seems to be a different denomination on every street corner. And new ones keep arising every day. Mostly because of theological differences and new forms of interpretation.

Which denomination do you associate yourself with? If so, why?

In 5:3-5 we see Paul suggesting that the congregation deliver a man over to his sin for living an immoral life. The reason to let him go on sinning was in hopes that he would repent and return to the church. Back then it was all about tough love. Sometimes we need to learn the hard way. The goal of church discipline should always be about repentance; not about getting even with a person.

Have you ever given up on someone in hopes of them learning on their own? If so, did they ever turn back?

In Chapter 8, Paul dives into whether or not you are allowed to eat meat that has been sacrificed to an idol first. That seems kind of strange to us, but in the pagan cultures of the time, almost all meat was sacrificed to various idols/ cultural gods. So it was definitely a valid question. Paul shows us that it was a matter of conscience more than anything.

How can you apply this teaching to our culture today? (For ex. regarding music, smoking, modesty, tattoos or yoga)

Chapter 11, deals with some controversial views toward women that do not seem relevant to our modern culture. One thing that you must take into account is that hair was very much lusted after back then. So in a modern sense, their hair was a modesty issue that we could compare to wearing skimpy clothing.

The real principle that Paul is showing here doesn't have to do with hair at all, but rather who is the head of the household. He places rules on hair in order to tell the difference between men and women. There are two different highly debated views on headship today:

Complementarian View:
God has made men and women as equals, but they each have different roles that complement each other.

Egalitarian View:
We are all the same no matter what. Women can do everything that a man can do.

Which view do you agree with? Why?

I believe that either way you look at it, it is pretty clear that men and women complement each other. I am terrible at many things that most women are good at, and I am great at a few things that some women are terrible at. That doesn't mean one is better than the other. We have the same value in God's sight. Our roles just tend to be different.

The Corinthians were highly influenced by a Greek mindset when it came to the role of their bodies. They thought spirituality was one thing and your body was another. One was good; one was evil. The two never crossed. Many believers today have the same Greek mindset when it comes to spiritual gifts that involve an outward act. We want to worship inwardly, but when it comes to a manifestation of the Spirit we get freaked out for some reason.

What do you know about spiritual gifts?

There are four main views on spiritual gifts today:

Cessationist:

Spiritual gifts were only for the early church and are not relevant today.

Continuationist:

Spiritual gifts are for today, but the "sign" gifts need to be looked at and tested with caution.

Charismatic:

Spiritual gifts are for every generation, and they should be practiced today. This view is limited by Scripture with no additions to the Word.

Hyper Charismatic:

Spiritual gifts are for every generation and contemporary revelations are equal to Scripture.

Which view on spiritual gifts do you associate with? Why?

The main places in the Bible that we learn about spiritual gifts are from 1 Corinthians 12-14, Romans 12, and Ephesians 4. Some people look at those lists and limit the gifts to them. Since we do not have a complete list it can be fairly unclear as to what all of the gifts are, which in turn, creates much disagreement in the church. One big mistake is to deny spiritual gifts all together. Another mistake is to pick one and think that it's better than the others.

CHU

SPIRITUAL GIFTS

THE SPIRITUAL GIFTS LISTED IN THOSE THREE MAIN SCRIPTURES ARE:

Romans 12:

Prophecy, Service, Teaching, Encouragement, Giving, Leadership, and Mercy.

Ephesians 4:

Apostleship, Prophecy, Evangelism, Pastor, and Teacher.

1 Corinthians 12:

Word of Wisdom, Word of Knowledge, Faith, Healing, Miracles, Prophecy, Discernment, Tongues and Interpreting tongues.

OVERVIEW OF SPIRITUAL GIFTS:

- Spiritual gifts are not to be confused with natural talent.
- Every Christian has at least one spiritual gift, if not multiple.
- No Christian has every spiritual gift.
- Spiritual gifts can be abused.
- The Holy Spirit chooses which gifts each of us receive.
- God's will is not accomplished if love is not the main motivation behind the gifts.

Describe a time when you feel like God used you, whether you knew it was your spiritual gift or not.

What is the purpose of spiritual gifts? (1 Peter 4:10-11)

THE BREAKDOWN

Prophecy:

Prophecy is the ability to speak truth into an individual's destiny and to reveal future events to the church in order to call for repentance or build them up. People with this gift can easily read others and "just know" things before they happen.

Service:

Service is the ability to meet physical needs within the body of Christ and apply a spiritual significance to it. People with this gift like to work behind the scenes and get joy out of helping others.

Teaching:

Teaching is the ability to apply Scripture in an easy-to-understand way. People with this gift love to study and are very focused on doctrinal application.

Encouragement:

Encouragement is the ability to motivate others on their faith journey. People with this gift are good counselors and can personally apply Scripture.

Giving:

Giving is the ability to earn money in order to meet the needs of others in a cheerful manner. People with this gift are good at making money and like to give behind the scenes.

Leadership:

Leadership is the ability to direct others in completing a God-given task or specific ministry work. People with this gift can clearly share a vision and others gladly follow their lead.

Mercy:

Mercy is the desire to take care of those that are going through difficult times without expecting anything in return. People with this gift enjoy one-on-one serving and are able to sympathize naturally.

Apostleship:

Apostles are those that have a desire to be sent out to start churches and ministries in the local community and around the world. People with this gift are comfortable in other cultures and able to execute a specific vision.

Evangelism:

Evangelists are those that can easily share the gospel with unbelievers and lead them to a personal relationship with Jesus Christ. People with this gift are very personable and convincing of the Truth.

Pastor:

Pastors are those that can guide, counsel, protect, and disciple a group of believers. Many times this gift is joined with the gift of teaching. People with this gift are great leaders and have a heart for discipleship.

Wisdom:

Wisdom is the ability to look at a situation and advise the best strategy for action based on the insight given. People with this gift can see various outcomes and can discern which one is the best to take.

Knowledge:

Knowledge is the ability to understand the Word and make it relevant to the church or specific situations. This gift includes supernatural words of knowledge that are to be used in serving others. People with this gift are able to seek out truth in the Bible and typically have unusual insight into situations or a person's life.

Faith:

Faith is the ability to have an overly confident belief that God will accomplish the impossible despite reality. People with this gift trust God completely and act in confidence.

Healing:

Healing is the ability to be used as a vessel by God in order to cure sickness and restore health back to normal. People with this gift are able to demonstrate the power of God through prayer, the laying on of hands or a spoken word.

Miracles:

Miracles is the ability to be used as a vessel for God to reveal His power through supernatural acts that alter the natural realm. Miracles are most often used to authenticate the gospel message. People with this gift speak truth with confidence and have it authenticated by a supernatural act.

Discernment (Distinguishing of Spirits):

Discernment is the ability to perceive what is from God through the discernment of good and evil spirits. People with this gift can easily tell what is from God and what is counterfeit.

Tongues:

There are three different types of tongues: One is a private prayer language (1 Cor 14:14-15), another is the ability to speak out a divine message in a new language in order for the Body to be built up, and the third is an entire language as a gift, which is to be used for missionary work.

Interpreting of Tongues:

Interpreting of tongues is the ability to translate a language that the hearer doesn't know, whether it is a real language or a heavenly language.

Can you think of a way to exercise your gift(s) in order to grow in it/them?

What impacted you the most in our study of 1 Corinthians?

When reading 1 Corinthians 12-14, you most likely recognized the infamous love chapter that was placed right in the middle. Paul does that deliberately to teach that loving others is the main focus behind every spiritual gift. If you are exercising your gifts for any other reason, you might as well not even use them. Love should be the reason behind everything.

How could you show love to those around you through your gifts?

CORINTHIANS

REASON

Second Corinthians was written by Paul as a defense of himself in response to the group of "super apostles." He wanted to encourage them in their offering for Jerusalem and to remind them of their victory in Christ.

THEME

Victory in Christ.

KEY VERSE

"But thanks be to God, who in Christ always leads us in triumphal procession, and through us spreads the fragrance of the knowledge of him everywhere." (2:14 ESV)

SECTIONS

Paul's Defense of Himself (Ch 1-7), The Poor in Jerusalem (Ch 8-9), Paul's Attack on Others (Ch 10-13)

KEY WORDS

Comfort, Affliction, Confidence, Weakness

THE BOOK

While the first letter to the Corinthians dealt with practical issues within the church, the second letter deals with personal insults that forced Paul to stand up for himself.

We know that a group of "super apostles" came into Corinth once Paul left, and they tried to take over by building themselves up and pushing Paul down. We don't know who they were exactly, but the content suggests that they were Jewish.

Some of the attacks on his character were that he wasn't bold enough, that he didn't care for the Corinthians since he was in a different city, that he wasn't a good speaker and that he wasn't even qualified to be teaching them such things. The "super apostles" knew that if they attacked Paul, his message would be thrown out as well.

Explain a time when you have had someone attack your character.

THE BOOK

While the first letter to the Corinthians dealt with practical issues within the church, the second letter deals with personal insults that forced Paul to stand up for himself.

We know that a group of "super apostles" came into Corinth once Paul left, and they tried to take over by building themselves up and pushing Paul down. We don't know who they were exactly, but the content suggests that they were Jewish.

Some of the attacks on his character were that he wasn't bold enough, that he didn't care for the Corinthians since he was in a different city, that he wasn't a good speaker and that he wasn't even qualified to be teaching them such things. The "super apostles" knew that if they attacked Paul, his message would be thrown out as well.

Explain a time when you have had someone attack your character:

How did you handle it?

Paul, does a good job at handling himself in such a crazy situation. He begins the letter in a very sincere way and encourages them in their walk. Around Chapter 9 he gets a little upset though and starts to attack them for going against his teaching. Sometimes a little heat is necessary.

Right in the middle of his encouragement and defense, Paul includes a large section on collecting money to give to the poor in Jerusalem. What?! We know from the past that Paul has a major heart for the poor so that makes sense, but doesn't that seem a little random? Well the Corinthians knew the importance of love, considering the whole chapter on it in his previous letter to them. It was a part of the gospel and therefore a part of their life. The "super apostles" weren't teaching love. They were attacking Paul and focusing on the negative instead. Paul knew that if he focused on loving others through donating to the poor then they would turn towards the truth. And this approach worked because we know that his third visit to Corinth was a joyous one.

What are some ways that you can better serve the poor?

GIFTED SAINTS

FINAL THOUGHTS

The application for these books is a little different than normal. Your job is to pray over the list of Spiritual Gifts this week and ask God to show you which ones He has personally chosen for you. You could also take a Spiritual Gifts inventory online. Once you are confident in your results, come up with some ways to begin exercising your gifts in your day-to-day life. Have fun with it! Remember…these are gifts God handpicked for you. He loves you and wants to share that love through you.

GALATIANS

AUTHOR

The letter to the Galatians was written by the apostle Paul. He is the perfect person to write on the topic of freedom from the Law because of his past as a fully devoted Jew. He knew about freedom in Christ alone more than anyone.

DATE

The dating of Galatians is highly debated. Some people believe that it was written early on as the first book in the New Testament, around AD 48, while others put the dating around AD 55.

If you believe Paul was writing to northern Galatia from Ephesus the later date would make the most sense. On the other hand, if you believe Paul was writing to southern Galatia from Antioch, the earlier date, before the Jerusalem Council, would fit your view.

AUDIENCE

Whether you believe Galatians was written to the northern or southern part, we can agree that it was written to the churches of Galatia.

REASON

Paul was teaching the Galatians to be free from the Law because there were Judaizers and false teachers telling them otherwise.

THEME

Freedom through Christ alone.

KEY VERSE

"For freedom Christ has set us free; stand firm therefore, and do not submit again to a yoke of slavery." (5:1 ESV)

SECTIONS

Personal (Ch 1-2), Doctrinal (Ch 3-4), Practical (Ch 5-6)

KEY WORDS

Christ, Freedom, Circumcision, Law

THE BOOK

The vibe of Galatians is much more negative compared to most of Paul's other letters because of how serious he feels about being set free from the Law. There is no joking around with him on that matter. Freedom is everything.

The Jewish people were being strangled by the Law. There was no way to fulfill it, but they still did their best to gain God's approval. The most important ritual that a Jewish male could ever do was become circumcised. It was mandatory back then and still is today in Jewish culture. It is a commandment from God!

Historically, why do Jews get circumcised? (Gen 17:10-14)

Paul is showing them that they no longer need to be circumcised in order to be saved, because Jesus' seed was the fulfillment of the circumcision covenant. His main focus is showing the Jewish people that there is truly nothing they can do physically in order to become saved. It's all about grace. They didn't get it though because for their entire lives the thought of having to work for your salvation has been drilled into their heads.

Insert: The Jerusalem Council.
Do you remember what happened in the JC? (Acts 15)

The main issue that we are dealing with here is whether salvation is received by faith or works. Paul is saying that it is by faith alone. A love like that was incomprehensible to the Jews. Quite frankly it's incomprehensible to most believers today. Many of whom still believe that going to heaven is about being a "good person". That's a risky subject if you ask me. Because then I would have to ask the question: How good do you have to be to go to heaven? What's the measurement?

The gospel is truly scandalous. God's love doesn't make sense to the normal individual, but once you understand the gift is freely given, it makes it easier to accept it.

Galatians 2:20 says, "I have been crucified with Christ. It is no longer I who live, but Christ who lives in me. And the life I now live in the flesh I live by faith in the Son of God, who loved me and gave himself for me" (ESV). **What do you think Paul meant when he said it was no longer he who lived, but rather Christ who lived in him? How can you apply that to your own life?**

Paul isn't done with talking about the Law yet, so he jumps right back in. **What was the purpose of the Mosaic Law that Moses received from God in Exodus and Leviticus?**

People crave simple plans. They want a checklist of things to follow in order to insure their reward will come, which just so happens to be a similar mindset in many churches today. They want to know what they can and cannot do in order to one day go to heaven. Guess what, it's not all about one day getting to heaven. When you become a new creation the focus of your life should shift to bringing heaven here, now. But, for some reason many denominations struggle with that understanding and provide the consumer with their desires instead. Following rules to get into heaven is a great business model; it's just far from the truth because now an actual relationship with Christ is put on the backburner or never even taught in the first place.

What rules do you see Christians placing on themselves today?

Instead of getting so caught up in what we should and shouldn't do, I believe that we need to redirect our attention to our identity in Christ and who God says we are. Galatians 4:6-7 says, "And because you are sons, God has sent the Spirit of His Son into our hearts, crying, 'Abba! Father!' So you are no longer a slave, but a son, and if a son, then an heir through God" (ESV).

Because of what Jesus did, you are an heir to the throne and have received the exact same inheritance that Jesus received. This. Is. HUGE. That means God blesses YOU the same way that He blessed His Son, JESUS. With salvation, providing for our needs, understanding the Father's heart, joy, gifts, communication with God, answered prayers, etc. Our inheritance was already paid for so God is literally just waiting for you to accept it. He gets joy out of blessing you. So take it in!

How have you seen God's blessing on your life? How can you better walk in this new understanding?

Some people may be wondering what that means to accept the blessing of the Father. It's as simple as asking Him for it and accepting your new identity. You are royalty. You are a son or daughter of the living God. LEGALLY. No ifs, ands, or buts. So look at yourself that way. Maybe you need to tell yourself that every day while looking in the mirror until it sticks. Seriously, DO IT. Your Father loves you and wants to bless you.

New identity brings new fruit. In Chapter 5, Paul shares with us that God calls humanity to interact with others while bearing what he calls the fruit of the Holy Spirit. The fruit is produced by nine characteristics that empower an individual to live a strong Christian life, displaying the love of Christ in every relationship.

What are the nine characteristics of the fruit of the Holy Spirit? (Gal 5:22)

Notice that it isn't nine different fruits that Paul talks about. A lot of people make that mistake. It's one fruit; nine characteristics. They are all needed in order to bear the fruit of the Holy Spirit. By self-reflecting on your life and looking at how the Holy Spirit is working through you, it is a great way to see your spiritual growth. You will know that you are on the right track when all characteristics of the fruit are present in your life.

While looking at the fruit in Galatians 5:22, which areas do you need to improve on? What can you do to become better in those areas? (John 15:4)

Whereas society shows us that our identity is based on the way that we look externally, God's focus is always on the internal and the work of the Holy Spirit. You are now an heir through God and have been set free from religion. Your new position calls for relationship instead. So take advantage of that!

HEIR
HEIRR
HEIRR
HEIRR
HEIR

Galatians 2:16 says, "We know that a person is not justified by works of the law but through faith in Jesus Christ, so we also have believed in Christ Jesus, in order to be justified by faith in Christ and not by works of the law, because by works of the law no one will be justified" (ESV).

How does that influence the way that you live your life?

AUTHOR

The letter to the Ephesians was written by the apostle Paul.

DATE

Paul wrote Ephesians around AD 60 to 62, during his Roman imprisonment. It can be assumed that Paul wrote from there because he was only on house arrest while in Rome, which meant that he had the freedom to preach and his friends were still able to visit him.

AUDIENCE

Paul wrote this letter to the church at Ephesus in Asia Minor and was to be used as a circulatory letter to all of the churches in the area.

Ephesus was a rough city. They were overly saturated with pagan idol worship and would do anything possible to acquire salvation. Even so, the Ephesian church had a strong foundation.

REASON

The reason that Paul wrote this letter was to teach them about identity and to show them how to stand firm by loving one another in their current culture.

THEME

Walking in your new identity.

KEY VERSE

"For we are His workmanship, created in Christ Jesus for good works, which God prepared beforehand, that we should walk in them." (2:10 ESV)

SECTIONS

Identity in Christ (Ch 1-3), Walking it Out (Ch 4-6)

KEY WORDS

In Christ, Walk, Body, Armor

THE BOOK

Paul begins Ephesians by saying, "Long before he laid down earth's foundations, he had us in mind, had settled on us as the focus of his love, to be made whole and holy by his love. Long, long ago he decided to adopt us into his family through Jesus Christ…He wanted us to enter into the celebration of his lavish gift-giving by the hand of his beloved Son" (1:4-6 MSG). There is so much about our new identity in this little section alone! We have been adopted. We are to be made whole and holy. His desire is to bless us. Those are all amazing things!

What does it mean to be adopted into the Kingdom?

What does it mean to be made whole and holy?

Do you understand that God wants to bless you with gifts just because you are now an heir to the throne? You don't have to do anything, it's just part of His character. **Spend a few minutes meditating on this and then write down what you sense God saying to you:**

Paul also uses the word predestination in describing us, which is a highly debated concept today. To predestine means to "determine an outcome or course of events in advance by divine will or fate" (Oxforddictionaries.com). There are two main views on predestination: Calvinism and Arminianism.

Do you have any thoughts on predestination before we look at them?

Calvinism, is the belief that we were chosen for salvation. God chooses who He wants to be in the Kingdom and all of life is worked out in order for His plan to come to fruition. Calvinists preach largely that everything in life happens for a reason.

Arminianism, on the other hand, is the belief that we were chosen to serve God. In this view, your faith is conditional and your future destiny is based on your actions now. They believe in free-will, but once you have chosen to follow Him, God has a predestined plan for your life.

You can find out more about each view online and make up your mind from there.

Paul says in 2:6 that once we are saved, Jesus "raised us up with him and seated us with him in the heavenly places" (ESV). That means we are seated up there with him right now. We have dual citizenship as citizens of heaven and of earth. Having a heavenly perspective should change the way that you go about your day. It's now about bringing the Kingdom into each of our situations. That means we can be confident in whatever comes our way because we are already victorious with Christ.

Which citizenship do you tend to view life from? What are some things you can do to have more of a heavenly perspective?

Do you remember the key verse from earlier?

Ephesians 2:10 says, "For we are his workmanship, created in Christ Jesus for good works, which God prepared beforehand that we should walk in them" (ESV).

Yes, we are saved by grace through faith, but that also means that we were created for good works. Faith results in works. They go together. He expects us to bless those around us, to make disciples, to pray for our friends, to lay hands on the sick, to cast out demons, and to walk in love constantly.

What are some ways that you can bless those around you?

KINGDOM

HEAVENLY PLACES

EARTH

Paul tells us to be imitators of God in Chapter 5. In other words, our lives should reflect Jesus. That means it is our job to bring the kingdom of God into our everyday life. Some people have such a hard time trying to figure out what the will of God is. I believe that the overarching will of God, after we receive His Son, is to bring heaven to earth and to ruin the works of the devil every day (1 John 3:8b). That's it!

How can you ruin the works of the devil in your daily life?

In Chapter 6, Paul describes the Armor of God and teaches us the keys to success regarding spiritual warfare.

Have you ever dealt with spiritual warfare before? What happened?

The battle that we are in is not in the natural realm, but in the spiritual. We can fight in confidence though, because we are already victorious in Christ.

Since we have been given the Holy Spirit and spiritual armor, we have everything we need to fight. But the issue is whether or not we know how to use it. As Paul looks at one of the Roman guards keeping watch over his house, he begins comparing their outfit to what we need in the spiritual realm.

The Belt of Truth:
The belt of the Roman uniform was used to hold everything together. Therefore, seeking out truth is what holds your life together. Jesus said, "I am the Way, and the TRUTH, and the Life" (John 14:6 ESV). If you seek after Jesus you will know how to dodge Satan, the father of lies.

The Breastplate of Righteousness:
A soldier's breastplate protected their heart and organs from being punctured. Righteousness is a gift that is attached to our new identity in Christ and we must be confident in the fact that we are no longer wicked in order to stop Satan's lies from entering our hearts.

The Shoes of Peace:
As believers in Jesus, we have peace with God and are to walk in peace with others everywhere we go.

The Shield of Faith:
Roman shields were made out of damp wood, covered in leather to extinguish flaming darts of the enemy. They were very large so that a soldier could protect his entire

body by hiding behind it. We must hide behind our faith and believe the promises of God.

The Helmet of Salvation:

The helmet protected the head, but more importantly the mind. Our salvation should give us confidence to block out false teachings and to live from our new nature instead of our old, sinful ways.

The Sword of the Spirit:

The sword was used in battle against the enemy. Our spiritual sword is the Word of God, the most powerful piece of weaponry available. When Jesus was tempted in the desert for 40 days, every response to Satan was to declare a verse and hold true to it. We must do the same. But this doesn't come naturally. We have to be trained in how to use the sword and then practice, practice, practice. That's why I'm so proud of you for going on this journey through the Word with me.

One thing to notice when looking at our armor is that there isn't a piece of armor for your back. That means you must never retreat. You are fighting from a place of victory!

Which pieces of armor do you need to daily start putting on or taking up? Put together a plan for doing so:

Above all, Paul says that we must continue praying in the Spirit. You need protection, but you also need prayer. Prayer helps us in standing firm against the enemy's attacks.

So, the full armor of God consists of truth, righteousness, the gospel, faith, salvation, the Word of God, and prayer. Every one of those pieces of armor are necessary in living a victorious Christian life.

Remember: You are fighting a spiritual battle; not a physical one. You have the power of Christ inside of you so there is no problem too big for Him to handle. Fight in God's strength! Fight with confidence! Fight from victory!

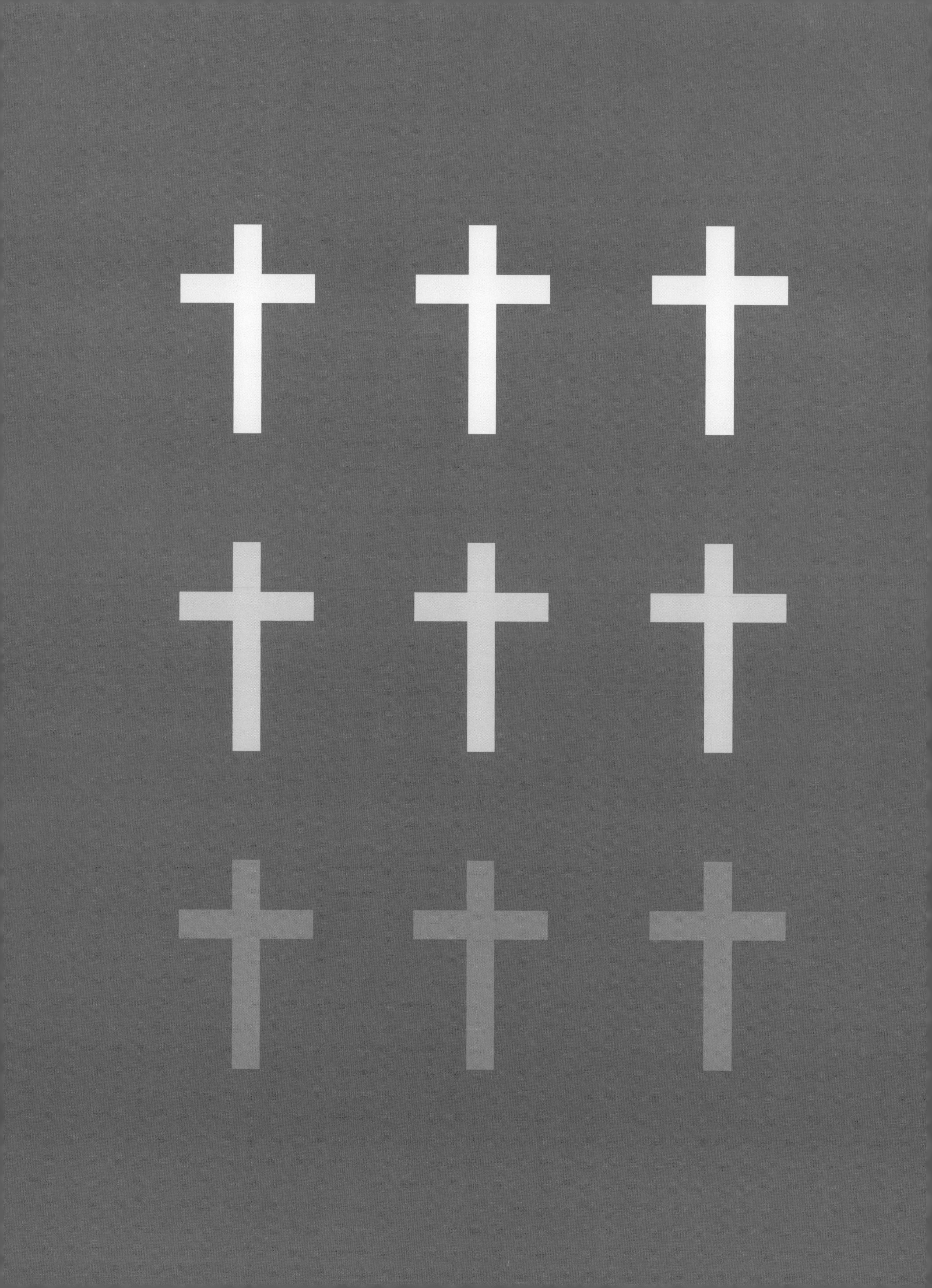

FINAL THOUGHTS

This week's application is a little different than normal since so many questions during the study were applicable to today.

I hereby challenge you to read Ephesians 6:10-20 every morning for one week straight with the confidence you have from your new "victorious" mindset. Then write out how you feel at the end of the week; sharing stories of breakthrough, newfound joy, or assurance of the power that lies within you.

PHILIPPIANS

AUTHOR

The letter to the Philippians was written by the apostle Paul.

DATE

Philippians was written around AD 61-62 towards the end of Paul's Roman imprisonment.

AUDIENCE

Paul was writing to the church in Philippi that consisted mainly of a Gentile audience.

REASON

Philippians was written to warn the Philippians about false teachings that were creeping into the church and to encourage them to remain joyful in the Lord.

THEME

Joy in the Lord.

KEY VERSE

"Rejoice in the Lord always; again I will say, rejoice!" (4:4 ESV)

SECTIONS

Meaning of True Life (Ch 1), Example of True Life (Ch 2), Goal of True Life (Ch 3), Walking out of True Life (Ch 4)

KEY WORDS

Gospel, Christ, Joy, Think

THE BOOK

The letter to the Philippians can be put in the category of "Prison Epistles", alongside Ephesians, Colossians, and Philemon. Philippians was written after those three as Paul was ending his stint under Roman house arrest. Paul had been told of issues among the Philippians by a gentleman named Epaphroditus who was sent to Paul as somewhat of a housekeeper. This letter was a response to those issues and a promise that Epaphroditus would be sent home soon.

Early on in Paul's letter we get the infamous quote "For to me, to live is Christ and to die is gain" (1:21 ESV). Paul is eager to go to heaven, but he's willing to stay because he loves people that much. Obviously God wants him to stick around since he came so close to death on all of his journeys but never ended up dying.

What does the statement "to live is Christ" mean? How can you go about doing that?

The biggest problem that the Philippians were dealing with, was disunity within the church. Pride and jealousy were seeping into the areas of blessings and spiritual gifts. Some people were becoming jealous that they weren't receiving the same spiritual gifts as others and that caused resentment among the group.

Explain a time when you were jealous of something another believer had that you didn't have:

In reality, the Body of Christ, the Church, is one. So when one person receives a gift, we all receive that gift, since we are in the same Body. We should be rejoicing over every blessing that our fellow brothers and sisters receive, not become jealous. And besides, who says God wouldn't give that gift again? Remember...it's the Spirit who apportions to each one individually as He wills.

Paul tells them to "imitate me" because he was so much like Christ. He's not being cocky like we would assume after reading that; he's just confident in who he was. He's imitating Christ so that's what the Philippians should be doing. He's their tangible evidence of someone following Christ and properly walking in their new identity.

In what way can you imitate Paul today?

Verses 2:5-8 are kind of the climax of the book, if you will. Paul looks at Christ's choice to empty himself in order to be like us so that he could save us.

When it says that Jesus "emptied" himself, what do you think that means?

That does not mean that Jesus was no longer fully God. He was both fully God and fully man the entire time. He gave up his power, not his nature, in order to be an example for us regarding what is possible with the Holy Spirit dwelling inside us.

In Chapter 4, Paul begins to fire-off a bunch of different commands to the Philippians. It seems that they were all last minute thoughts that he had to get on the page before the letter was sent off. This is also where we see the key verse, "Rejoice in the Lord always; again I will say, rejoice!" (4:4 ESV). That's a huge command if you really think about it and most of us would struggle with fulfilling it every day.

What does it mean to rejoice always? How is that even possible?

In which areas of your life do you struggle with remaining joyful?

Finding joy in many situations can be difficult, especially considering the way the world is heading. Another tough one is remaining peaceful in a world where there is so much disagreement and disunity. Paul says that the peace of God will guard your heart and mind if you control your thoughts and remain thankful.

What does Paul tell us to think about in 4:8? How can you obey that personally?

Focusing on the positive in every situation allows us to be more joyful people. There are many studies that show how negative thoughts create toxins in our brain and force it to function improperly. On the other hand, when you focus on good things, your brain works the way that it was created to. If we are to restore our minds to fullness, we must begin with our "thought life".

Do you typically tend to look at the positives or negatives in situations? What are some ways that you can turn negative situations into positive ones?

Paul makes it clear that joy and peace are dependent on what we choose to think about. I don't know about you, but I love being joyful and peaceful so I try to remain focused on everything on that list. To think about anything else is actually going against our new nature. Every day we have the choice to renew our mind through Scripture in order to be transformed and to have a kingdom mentality instead of an earthly one.

ONE BODY

ONE BODY

ONE MIND

ONE CHURCH

ONE GOD

ONE GOD

ONE MIND

ONE CHURCH

ONE BODY

ONE MIND

ONE CHURCH

ONE GOD

ONE BODY

ONE BODY

ONE MIND

ONE CHURCH

ONE GOD

ONE GOD

ONE MIND

ONE CHURCH

ONE BODY

ONE MIND

ONE CHURCH

ONE GOD

FINAL THOUGHTS

"Zach, how are you happy all of the time? I don't get it. Do you ever have a bad day?" To which I always respond "Nope. Just am!"

I can recall one or two bad days in the past few years. Before that, it had been a while. One of the times I had just been let go of one of my jobs because they were bought out, a side project I was working on wasn't turning out as I had hoped, and I had no direction for where to go from there. I remember sitting in my car outside of Starbucks talking to my buddy Geoff about it. I had never felt so lost in my life. If you know me, I always have a plan. But this time, I didn't.

Then, the next day, I was back to my normal self. Having a good day as usual.

I truly believe that you can have a good day every day. Many people think I'm crazy for believing that. Maybe it's just some hippy mindset that I have, but really, I believe it's possible, and I believe you can, too.

As you know, Paul spent a lot of time in jail. People weren't too keen on him causing a scene in their city by talking about Jesus and disrupting business, so they would just send him off in shackles. Wouldn't you think after the first or second time that you'd quiet down a little bit? He didn't. He just brushed off his shoulder and kept on going.

If it weren't for his prison sentences then we wouldn't have the "Prison Epistles", so I'm alright with it. Honestly, what else would you do while in prison, but write motivational letters to churches to tell them to keep doing the same thing that you're currently in jail for? Duh.

It's wild though because this whole letter is filled with him being in constant joy and he mentions a ton of times that they should rejoice because life is wonderful. Paul believed that no matter what happened in his life, it would all be used for a higher purpose. If he was in jail, he could work with it. If he was having "the worst day ever" in a normal person's life, he could work with it. Paul was joyous no matter what happened in his life because he knew God was always looking out for him.

And so that's where I'm at. You want to know how I can have a good day every day no matter what I'm put through? It's because my joy comes from knowing Jesus. That's it. Nothing more, nothing less.

In what ways can changing your outlook on life help you navigate your current circumstances?

COLOSSIANS

AUTHOR

The letter to the Colossians was written by the apostle Paul.

DATE

Paul wrote Colossians at the same time as Ephesians and Philemon around AD 60-61, during the beginning of his Roman imprisonment.

AUDIENCE

This letter was written to the church at Colossae which was made up of mostly Gentiles.

REASON

Colossians was written to correct some false teachings that were distorting the Colossians view of Jesus, to show them the full deity of Christ, and to show their fullness in Christ.

THEME

Fullness in Christ.

KEY VERSE

"For in him all the fullness of Deity dwells in bodily form, and in him you have been made complete, and He is the Head over all rule and authority." (2:9-10 NASB)

SECTIONS

Fullness of Christ (Ch 1-2), New Life in Christ (Ch 3-4)

KEY WORDS

Fullness, Wisdom, Knowledge, Faith

THE BOOK

As we learned when looking at Ephesians and Philemon, Paul was under Roman house arrest at the time of this writing. While during house arrest, he could have visitors and live somewhat freely, all the while chained to a Roman soldier.

A man named Epaphras, who was part of the church in Colossae, reported to Paul that things were going badly. Paul had no real authority over the Colossians, but he did his best to redirect their focus, in order to understand their new self/identity in Christ.

A large portion of Colossians matches the content in Ephesians so we don't have too many new topics to look at in this book. It also helps that Paul writes to them in a very straight-forward way, so that they understand it.

False teachings were taking place amongst the church in Colossae because they felt that there was no way Christianity could be so simple. Therefore they made it hard. They added different rules and regulations to their doctrine, which took away from the simplicity of the gospel and formed a religion instead. In reality, Jesus came to save us from religion.

The true gospel is Jesus plus nothing.

What do you add to your faith out of habit or from church pressure?

JESUS + NOTHING
JESUS + NOTHING
JESUS + NOTHING
JESUS + NOTHING
JESUS + NOTHING

There are countless additions. That's what makes Colossians so relevant to us today. When we spend our time adding tasks to the gospel, it causes Jesus to lose his authority. He is really the end-all, be-all. He is all we need.

By turning Christianity into a religion, what type of things do you miss out on? Intimacy with Jesus? Powerful time in prayer? The Spirit moving in your life?

God is looking for people who will live in the simplicity of the gospel and let the work of Jesus reign supreme in their lives. He wants to work with you on creating wholeness in every situation and every relationship you're involved in. He desires relationship; not religion.

One of the distinct characteristics of Colossians is that it is a great example of Christology (the study of Christ). Paul gives an in-depth analysis of who Christ was and is, and how he relates to us.

What are some of the characteristics of Christ that stood out to you while reading Colossians?

We have looked at it multiple times, but when we come into Christ, we become a completely new creation. Our old self is gone and our new self has taken over. The past has LITERALLY been forgotten because God loves you SO MUCH. There is no need to dwell in the old anymore. Christ is now living inside of us, and he wants to influence the lives of everyone around us. Sharing God's love and the good news about Jesus are our main purpose now that we have it. You may be the only Christian that the people around you come in contact with today, and Jesus wants to love them just as much as he loves you. Share it.

What are your favorite ways of sharing the love of Christ?

To go along with this new understanding of putting on your new self, we are going to draw it out in order to visualize it. First off, write out words inside of the "old self" outline below that you would have used to describe your old self.

THE OLD SELF IS GONE

Next, go back to your "old self" and color in the body with a black marker because all of those titles are no longer relevant. Now on the blank body below, write out all of the things that God says you are after having put on your new self. This is your true identity (see Ephesians 1 for starters).

**THE NEW SELF IS PUT ON.
THIS IS WHO I REALLY AM.**

THESSALONIANS

AUTHOR

The two letters to the Thessalonians were written by the apostle Paul. Silas and Timothy were present during the writing, but the doctrine was all his.

DATE

Paul wrote the first letter to the Thessalonians around AD 50-51 while in Corinth and the second letter was sent just a few months later.

AUDIENCE

The Thessalonians were a group of new believers who didn't get much formal training from Paul. They were both Jew and Gentile and had been brought up under pagan worship. We know that they were already being persecuted for their faith and were being sent false letters from "Paul" in order to sway them from the truth.

Where was Thessalonica?
Thessalonica was at the northernmost part of the Aegean Sea, and it was also along the Egnatian Way on land. It was in one of the best spots possible for starting a church in hopes of it's message being spread all over the Greco-Roman world. Business flourished there because of it's location. It was definitely the place to be.

Paul visited Thessalonica on his second journey after being led there by the Holy Spirit. We saw that story in Acts when the Holy Spirit blocked them from going to Asia, but Paul saw a man in his dream that told him to go to Macedonia. Thessalonica just so happened to be the capital city of Macedonia during the Roman empire.

A little while after establishing the church in Thessalonica, Paul was working in Corinth when he received a support letter from the Thessalonians. This first letter to the Thessalonians is in response to their gift.

FIRST LETTER

REASON

Paul wrote to encourage them to press on in their faith, to not listen to the false accusations against him and to keep working hard until the Second Coming.

THEME

In Expectation of Christ.

KEY VERSE

"Now may the God of peace Himself sanctify you completely, and may your whole spirit and soul and body be kept blameless at the coming of our Lord Jesus Christ." (5:23 ESV)

SECTIONS

Praise (Ch 1-3), Encouragement (Ch 4-5)

KEY WORDS/PHRASES

Gospel, Faith, Hope, Day of the Lord

THE BOOK

Paul starts off by commending them for living out their faith so well. You can tell that he is happy with the way that they have been doing things. Paul tends to be a professional motivator. He knows just what to say to get people to progress in their faith. And it works almost every time because they know that he truly cares about them and does it from a place of love. Paul also focused more on their holiness than on themselves.

Who is the most motivating person that you know? What is it about them that motivates you?

The Thessalonians are taught to excel in love towards one another and to work hard so that they wouldn't be in need of anything. He says, "We urge you, brothers, to do this more and more, and to aspire to live quietly, and to mind your own affairs, and to work with your hands, as we instructed you, so that you may walk properly before outsiders and be dependent on no one" (4:10-12 ESV). Yikes. For some reason, work is a topic that is rarely discussed within the church today. In Genesis, God says that, because of the Fall, we will be forced to work and it won't be fun. Paul is continuing on with the same statement here. He is saying that if you are able to work, you should be making your own money and taking care of your responsibilities, not expecting to live off of other's money.

What are your views on work-ministry-life balance?

Would you consider yourself a hard worker? Do you view work as if you're "working for the Lord"?

Some people believe in the Rapture based on 1 Thess 4:13-18, do you have any views about the Rapture? Do you think God would remove believers from Earth before bringing judgment? (we will look at this more when studying Revelation)

As Paul shows in 5:11, one of the best ways to share the love of Jesus to those around you is through encouragement and speaking truth into their lives. The sanctification process is currently bringing your heart in line with the Father's heart more so every day. That means you will be able to see people the way God sees them and share how He feels about them. That's amazing! We can partner with God in building up people that He loves. That goes for believers and unbelievers alike. Encouraging each others' gifts increases our confidence in what God gave us. It can also allow us to push boundaries and grow in our own spiritual life.

Who are some people that you want to encourage? In what ways will you be able to?

Chapter 5 is packed with a bunch of unrelated goodies that Paul wanted to tell them before closing out the letter. He says that it is God's will for us to rejoice, pray, and be thankful at all times.

How good of a job are you doing with those three commands? How can you improve?

Then, he says not to quench the Spirit and not to despise prophetic utterances, but to examine them carefully. Both are very important things. Many times we can be extra skeptical towards prophecies, especially in the U.S., because they aren't a commonly taught subject. But, the New Testament consistently shows that prophecy is a major part of the Christian life. That sure is something to pray about. Let God speak to you about His heart towards this subject.

Think of some ways we tend to quench the Spirit in our lives:

And that's that. Paul is a happy man in this first letter to the Thessalonians, and he shares some great insight about the Christian walk and the Second Coming.

YOU GOT THIS
DON'T GIVE UP
KEEP GOING
I BELIEVE IN YOU
GODS' GOT YOU

YOU GOT THIS
DON'T GIVE UP
KEEP GOING
I BELIEVE IN YOU
GODS' GOT YOU

SECOND LETTER

THESSALONIANS

REASON

Paul wrote to comfort the Thessalonians from affliction and false teaching regarding the Second Coming.

THEME

Comfort until the Second Coming.

KEY VERSE

"Since indeed God considers it just to repay with affliction those who afflict you, and to grant relief to you who are afflicted as well as to us, when the Lord Jesus is revealed from heaven with his mighty angels." (1:6-7 ESV)

SECTIONS

Perseverance (Ch 1), The Future (Ch 2-3)

KEY WORDS

Coming of Christ, Affliction, Man of Lawlessness, Faith, Day of the Lord

THE BOOK

Second Thessalonians is far different from Paul's first letter to the Thessalonians even though they were written only a few months apart. Paul now seems to be very distant from them and upset over something that was reported to him shortly after the first letter was sent.

He starts off with complimenting them, but quickly gets into the heavy stuff. The Thessalonians had received a false letter from "Paul" saying that the Second Coming was just around the corner so there is no need to work or press-on in their faith anymore. The sad thing is that many people believed it. And that made Paul furious.

He goes on to say that it couldn't be close because the man of lawlessness had yet to make himself known, so they had a while.

What are some other names for the Antichrist? (Ps 10:2-4, 53:3, 74:8-10; Isa 10:5-12, 14:2,12; Dan 7:8, 9:27; Ezek 28:12; Jer 4:6-7; Rev 9:11; 2 Thess 2:3,8; Zec 11:16-17) **What do we know about him?**

Do you think the antichrist will rise up during your lifetime? Why or why not?

Paul continues on with his thoughts on work from the first letter and encourages them again to keep at it. He goes so far as to tell them not to even give any Christians food if they aren't willing to work…because they are lazy. A lot of the Thessalonians were doing just that since they were told that the Second Coming was just around the corner. I see that a lot today, not necessarily in the area of work, but definitely in the areas of evangelism and prayer. This should be anything but a time to slow down! We should be ramping up our evangelism and prayer lives more than ever if we truly believe that the Second Coming is approaching.

If you believe that to be true, what are some things that you can be praying for? And who could you share the good news about Jesus with?

Do you have a good enough understanding of Hell to make you want to evangelize? Or are you fine knowing some of the people around you will go there?

Rejoice
Pray
~~Complain~~
Be thankful

GOD
HAS

THE
ANS
WER

THE
ANS
WER

GOD
HAS

God created us to work alongside with Him. We aren't His robots. He actually desires us to be creative with Him and co-labor throughout the day. Whatever that looks like for your situation…it's different for everyone. It's such a privilege to get to work with our Father every day.

How can you bring the kingdom of God into your workplace?

Since God has the answer to all business solutions, drama, cures, etc, what kind of answers can you be praying for in your line of work?

FINAL THOUGHTS

It's interesting to note that the first two letters written in the New Testament were about the Second Coming. There has been a lot of talk about the topic lately and many people are wondering if it will happen during their lifetime. That would obviously be a GREAT thing for us, but a TERRIBLE thing for those around us that have yet to be saved. And it's our responsibility to share the gospel with them.

With that said, list three people that you want to evangelize to this year and outline a short plan for encouraging each of them:

TIMOTHY+TITUS

These three letters were written by Paul between his final missionary journey and the beginning of his second Roman Imprisonment. They are known as the "Pastoral Epistles" because Timothy and Titus were both placed in the pastoral position in different cities, and Paul is teaching them how to get their people in line. He knew that the church had to be in place before any evangelism was to happen. And we all know Paul's thoughts on evangelism: It was everything.

Even though they are called the "Pastoral Epistles," it was neither Timothy nor Titus's job to remain in each location as the pastor. Paul sent them to set things straight, but the main desire of his heart was for them to meet him in Rome before he was martyred.

Timothy was sent to deal with the leadership in Ephesus, but we know that he was a very timid man, making the task far outside of his comfort zone. Titus on the other hand was sent to Crete to deal with the church as a whole (elders and members), but he was strong and self-sufficient, which made Paul's job much easier.

Not only were these letters used as motivation and direction, but Paul knew that they would also be used as credentials to prove the authority of Timothy and Titus.

FIRST TIMOTHY

DATE

First Timothy was written around AD 64-66 from Nicopolis in Greece.

AUDIENCE

Paul wrote this letter to Timothy whom he loved so much that he considered him his own "son". He also trusted him more than anybody and encouraged Timothy to always press on through his timidity.

REASON

Paul wrote to encourage Timothy amidst opposition from false teachers and to instruct him on leadership within the church.

THEME

Leadership roles inside of the Church.

KEY VERSE

"I hope to come to you soon, but I am writing these things to you so that, if I delay, you may know how one ought to behave in the household of God, which is the church of the living God, a pillar and buttress of truth." (3:14-15 ESV)

SECTIONS

Order in the Church (Ch 1-3), Behavior in the Church (Ch 4-6)

KEY WORDS

Teach, Sound, Faith, Doctrine

SECOND TIMOTHY

DATE

Second Timothy was written around AD 67 just before Paul's martyrdom. Paul was back in prison in Rome at the time.

AUDIENCE

Timothy, Paul's "beloved son", was still located in Ephesus, and he was dealing with false teachers.

REASON

This is Paul's final epistle; in which he hands over the ministry responsibilities to Timothy. Paul encourages him to have sound doctrine and to stand strong against opposition that will come his way.

THEME

Finish strong, Timothy!

KEY VERSE

"As for you, always be sober-minded, endure suffering, do the work of an evangelist, fulfill your ministry" (4:5 ESV)

SECTIONS

Timothy's Faith (Ch 1), Stand Strong and Be Sound (Ch 2), Fighting False Teachers (Ch 3), Paul's Death in View (Ch 4)

KEY WORDS/PHRASES

Endure, Faith, Abide, Sound, Doctrine

THE BOOKS

From these letters and also from the book of Acts, we know that Timothy had a Greek father and a Jewish mother. His father may not have been around much, so Timothy had a Jewish upbringing by his mom and grandma. In Acts 16, Paul urged Timothy to get circumcised, not for a religious purpose, but in order to be allowed into the synagogue for evangelism purposes.

Paul sent Timothy to sort out all of the issues in Ephesus that could not be handled through a letter.

Based on our study of Ephesians, do you remember what was happening in Ephesus at the time? (Feel free to check your notes!)

Not only were things bad in Ephesus, but Christians in Rome were facing persecution by Nero at an alarming rate. Paul was in prison, but he knew his martyrdom was right around the corner. Therefore, it was time to hand things over to Timothy. Hence the reason why Paul is so adamant about Timothy continuing on in the faith and persevering until his mission is complete.

POWER
LOVE
SOUND MIND

Time and again, Paul had seen people backtrack in their faith when persecution began to heat up. Timothy was not going to be one of them if Paul had anything to do with it.

Do you know anybody that was a strong believer and ended up leaving the faith? What were their reasons?

Paul's advice was to keep pressing on, no matter what happened. He knew that it would all be worth it in the end even though Timothy was beginning to lose hope.

How do you stay strong when times get tough?

The biggest issue that Timothy was dealing with in Ephesus was poor leadership within the church. Paul told him that he needed to go in and replace the bad elders with good ones. Otherwise the church was going to fall apart. Calling people out for their wrongdoings must have been one of the hardest things for "timid Timothy" to ever do. But the gospel was far more important than Timothy's comfort.

Paul knew that if the leaders within the church were doing their job well, then the people would follow suit and model their lives after them. This all goes back to the repeated theme of many of Paul's letters: Foundation. A solid foundation is mandatory for spiritual growth...then and now.

Who do you model your life after? Why?

Paul breaks the leadership down to elders and deacons with their requirements attached. He doesn't stop at whether or not they are qualified, but he makes sure that Timothy looks at their character too. If you don't display a lifestyle of holiness outside of the church, what makes you think you can reflect holiness on the inside? Paul was looking for people that were solid in every aspect of their life.

What characteristics do you think good leaders have?

If the bad leaders remain in office for too long, the doctrine of the church might even be compromised. The most important thing for leaders to do today is to make sure that their doctrine is completely scriptural. That doesn't mean pulling one verse out of context and creating a new doctrine out of it either. All teaching must be in line with the Father's heart and confirmed in multiple places throughout the Bible.

If you are not on the leadership team of your home church, you have a responsibility of knowing the Word and calling out leaders that are straying from the truth. Being grounded in Scripture protects the Body from crumbling through false teaching. That's why I am so proud of you for going through this study and setting yourself up for success. Your church and everyone around you should be ecstatic. Knowing what God says to us and about us is the greatest thing we can ever focus our minds on.

Timothy was timid, but his calling overpowered what people said about him. The same thing goes for you today. Typically, your calling is something impossible in the eyes of society and is always in line with God's will. Good thing for you is that our God is the God of the impossible, and He almost always calls the unqualified. You aren't the first and you definitely aren't the last. Just as Paul is telling Timothy to press on through the "impossibilities", he is telling us the same thing. God likes to show-off through our lives. In so many cases we fail to recognize that though, because we have such a worldly mindset. If you keep your eyes on Him and acknowledge that He wants to use you for His divine tasks, you will soon realize what a privilege it is to work for your Dad every day.

always in line with God's will. Good thing for you is that our God is the God of the impossible, and He almost always calls the unqualified. You aren't the first and you definitely aren't the last. Just as Paul is telling Timothy to press on through the "impossibilities", he is telling us the same thing. God likes to show-off through our lives. In so many cases we fail to recognize that though, because we have such a worldly mindset. If you keep your eyes on Him and acknowledge that He wants to use you for His divine tasks, you will soon realize what a privilege it is to work for your Dad every day.

Do you sense God calling you to do something "impossible" (by human standards)? What is it? What is stopping you?

3 Remind them to be submissive to rulers and authorities, to be obedient, to be ready for every good work, [2] to speak evil of no one, to avoid quarreling, to be gentle, and to show perfect courtesy toward all people. [3] For we ourselves were once foolish, disobedient, led astray, slaves to various passions and pleasures, passing our days in malice and envy, hated by others and hating one another. [4] But when the goodness and loving kindness of God our Savior appeared, [5] he saved us, not because of works done by us in righteousness, but according to his own mercy, by the washing of regeneration and renewal of the Holy Spirit, [6] whom he poured out on us richly through Jesus Christ our Savior, [7] so that being justified by his grace we might become heirs according to the hope of eternal life. [8] The saying is trustworthy, and I want you to insist on these

DATE

Paul wrote to Titus at the same time as First Timothy, around AD 64-66 while in Nicopolis, Greece.

AUDIENCE

Titus was Paul's representative and he didn't need to have his hand held. He was strong and followed directions well, always finding a way to accomplish the given task. Paul had sent him to the island of Crete in order to get the members of the church there in line. Unlike Timothy, Titus was fully Greek and an uncircumcised believer.

REASON

Paul quickly touches on leadership and then teaches Titus how to teach godly living among members of the church in Crete.

THEME

Sound doctrine is everything.

KEY VERSE

"Therefore rebuke them sharply, that they may be sound in the faith" (1:13 ESV)

SECTIONS

Church Order (Ch 1), Sound Doctrine (Ch 2), Godly Living (Ch 3)

KEY WORDS/PHRASES

Be Sound, Good Deeds, Grace, Doctrine

TITUS

Notice how different the tone is in the letters to Timothy and Titus. Whereas Timothy was very timid, Titus was strong and self-sufficient. Paul knew that he could send Titus to perform a task, and he would find a way of getting it done. Titus didn't need his hand held at all and Paul knew it. He dropped him off on the island of Crete and had him get to work.

Crete was a bad place. It was similar to parts of Vegas today. Immorality at its finest. Titus was put in the thick of it, and although he was kind of in over his head, that didn't stop him from giving it a shot. Paul felt like he should write to encourage Titus and help him to deal with the immorality. Just as he did with Timothy, Paul told Titus what to do with the leadership, but his main focus was on the people since false teachings were beginning to creep into the Cretan's doctrine.

Paul, teaches the members how to act in order to keep the entire church in line. He focuses on two things: character and truth, both of which must be present in all members. Having a good character outside of the church and having a solid foundation in Scripture. Paul says that we are to adorn the gospel.

What do you think it means to adorn the gospel? In what ways can you adorn the gospel?

HOLD FIRMLY TO THE TRUTH

HOLD
FIRMLY
TO THE
TRUTH

Looking good to unbelievers is something that Paul addresses. Believers need to show unbelievers that what we have is better than what they have. We have the answers to all of life's problems. We have the Creator of the universe available, 24/7. I believe that the church really needs to improve in this area. We have separated ourselves so far from society that we often have no idea what would draw unbelievers in. Society portrays us as prude, boring, and hypocritical. Paul says that we must live up to what is good in society's eye and take that one step further. Our goodness and love should draw unbelievers in.

What virtues does our culture associate with "good people"? How can we live those out?

Ask God to point out anything in your life that might be holding you back from maturity, and then write them down below:

Now put together a "plan of attack" for how to deal with those roadblocks:

In 2:14, Paul commands the Cretans to be zealous for good works. Oxford Dictionaries describes "zeal" as, "great energy or enthusiasm in pursuit of a cause or an objective". We need to pursue good deeds with enthusiasm. Good deeds affect the world around us, and we can share the love of Jesus through them.

"Wait a second, I thought I was saved by grace not by works?"
Yes, that is true, but our salvation should now result IN good works every day, not FROM them.

Paul teaches Titus that his disciples MUST be producing fruit. All real believers produce fruit. That is part of the sanctification process. We get better over time, and God becomes more and more noticeable in our actions. If you aren't producing fruit and becoming godlier then there is something wrong in your spiritual life.

The Pastoral Epistles all focus on fighting for truth to reign supreme inside the church. Paul knew that if the foundation was strong, the building wouldn't collapse. There are many teachings infiltrating the church today that are just NOT biblical. We must fight for truth. Our lives should reflect the gospel, and it should be our desire to bring the kingdom everywhere we step.

False teachings/deception are only going to ramp up from here. I'm ready for it. Are you?

FINAL THOUGHTS

As you know from the introduction, I hit a point in my life where I was fed up with Christians around me. In reality, I was fed up with my hypocritical self.

I grew up in the church.
I spent a ton of time at Christian camps, even working at one for the summer.
I went to a Christian University.
I wrote Christian books.
But when it all came down to it I didn't really know what I believed. Yeah, I knew the basics but that was it.

One night, I was sitting in my basement, contemplating life and whether or not I could consider myself a Christian still. I thought about every other religion and how serious they take it. Jewish boys in Israel are required to have the entire Torah memorized by the time they are TWELVE. And what do we do? Take some confirmation classes for a season and we're good?

I couldn't have told you what 90% of the books in the Bible are about at that point. Yet I claimed to believe it with all of my heart. How ridiculous is that?!

So that's when I departed on my journey to Australia to spend 70 hours/week in the Bible for 9 months. Studying. Praying. Crying. Worshiping. Falling in love in a way that I didn't know was possible. The foundation that I built was as solid as concrete. There is nothing that can shake me now. I'm in too deep.

As we saw in Timothy and Titus, having a strong foundation is the most important thing we can do as false teaching continues to infiltrate the church.

What is your plan for building a stronger foundation?

PHILEMON

AUTHOR

The author of this letter to Philemon was the apostle Paul.

DATE

Paul wrote to Philemon at the same time as Ephesians and Colossians around AD 60-61, during his Roman imprisonment.

AUDIENCE

The letter to Philemon was obviously written to Philemon, but Paul also includes Apphia, Archippus, and their house church in Colossae in order to hold Philemon accountable for the content of the letter.

REASON

Paul wrote as an appeal for Philemon to forgive Onesimus for running away and to show that he was now useful in sharing the gospel.

THEME

Forgiveness, Equality, and Reconciliation in Christ.

KEY VERSE

"I appeal to you for my child Onesimus, whose father I became in my imprisonment." (10 ESV)

SECTIONS

Introduction (Ch 1-3), Praise for Philemon (Ch 4-7), Plea for Onesimus (Ch 8-20), Purpose (Ch 21-25)

KEY WORDS

Slave, Receive, Appeal, Love

THE BOOK

Philemon is the only personal letter of recommendation in the Bible.
So what is going on here that makes this book part of Scripture?

Well, back in the day, slavery was much different from what it is today and in the recent past. Whereas our views regarding slavery are all about disrespect and being treated poorly, being a slave in the Greco-Roman world was actually a decent profession. Neither the conditions or the money were bad and there were even more slaves than there were free people. It was a totally acceptable job in terms of conditions and money.

So here we have a man named Onesimus who was a slave of a man named Philemon. Onesimus had run away with a big bag of money, most likely while he was out running an errand for Philemon. We don't know exactly what happened, but we do know that the penalty for running away was death.

Check out the maps of Paul's journeys and locate where Colossae is.
Now find Rome. That's how far Onesimus ran so that he wouldn't be found by Philemon. It just so happens to be that while he was in Rome he was introduced to Paul who was on house arrest. During their time together Onesimus gave his life to Christ. Before Onesimus could go any further, Paul made him go back home and ask for forgiveness from Philemon. Yikes.

When you enter into life with Christ it doesn't mean that you can run from your past. Yes, you are forgiven and have been wiped clean, but it also gives you the opportunity to make your past right by bringing wholeness to your relationships or situations.

Did you need to reconcile any relationships once you became a Christian? How did it go?

I have a buddy who got into some serious trouble with the law before he became a Christian. The judge allowed him to go into a Christian sobriety program, per his parent's request, for a year in order to lessen his sentence. He agreed and now he is really on fire for the Lord. Although that doesn't change the fact that he still has to do some time in a state workhouse after the program. But, the situation changes when your mindset changes. In my opinion, he's being taken care of by the government in order to share the gospel with other guys who did some bad stuff too. It's all about the way you look at it. Just like Onesimus, my buddy has to go deal with his past before he can get a roll on the Lord's work for his life.

The good thing about the story with Onesimus and Philemon is that Paul actually knew Philemon, so he could send a letter to him explaining the situation. But that didn't mean that Onesimus was off the hook. His life was still in the hands of Philemon since the consequence of a runaway slave is death.

On top of it all, Paul was making Onesimus hand-deliver the letter. He had to walk nearly 1,500 miles, without knowing the outcome. This letter was literally life or death for him.

What do you think was going through his mind on this journey?

One of the coolest things about this story is that the name Onesimus means "useless". By sending him back with this letter, Paul is saying that he will now be useful to Philemon. He's a new creation completely. He has a purpose now. But first things first, he needs to get his relationships right.

What do you think it looked like when Philemon opened the door and Onesimus was standing there? Do you think Onesimus threw the letter at him and ran away until he had read it?

We know that Philemon handled it well because we still have the letter today. Forgiveness isn't an easy thing, but it can be the one thing that changes your life. God has forgiven you of your past and has given purpose to your formerly useless life, just like we see here with Onesimus.

I FORGIVE YOU.

journey

FINAL THOUGHTS

If you have hurt someone in the past or been hurt by someone, you may need to take an Onesimus journey of your own to make things right with them…even if it's difficult.

So for the application this week, spend some time thinking about whether you need to make that journey or not. If you do, reach out and either ask for forgiveness or forgive someone. If you don't, that decision could hold you back from a life of blessings.

Feel free to share the story below:

HEBREWS

AUTHOR

Nobody really knows who the author of Hebrews is, and, quite frankly, there are several possibilities: Luke, Paul, Barnabas, Apollos, or Priscilla and Aquilla. Understanding the content of the book is not based on your view of the authorship so do not get hung up on trying to figure it out.

DATE

The book of Hebrews was most likely written around AD 64-65. The Temple had yet to be destroyed, and Nero was just beginning his persecution of Christians.

AUDIENCE

The author of Hebrews directed his attention towards Hebrew believers that were turning their focus back to the religious nature of Judaism.

REASON

The book of Hebrews was written to show how Jesus and the New Covenant were superior to Judaism and the Law. The author also encouraged the Hebrew believers in their faith journey as they dealt with a new wave of persecution.

THEME

Jesus is better than Judaism.

KEY VERSE

"But in fact the ministry Jesus has received is as superior to theirs as the covenant of which he is mediator is superior to the old one, since the new covenant is established on better promises." (8:6 NIV)

SECTIONS

Jesus is Better than Angels (Ch 1-2), Jesus is Better than Moses and Joshua (Ch 3-4), Jesus is better than the Aaronic Priesthood ((Ch 5-7), Jesus is Better than the Old Covenant (Ch 8-10), Perseverance is Key (Ch 11-12), Conclusion (Ch 13)

KEY WORDS

Better, Covenant, Perfect, Faith

THE BOOK

Hebrews is not an easy book for many Gentile readers to get through, because of their lack of Old Testament knowledge. As I have said many times, it is CRUCIAL to put yourself in the shoes of the reader as best you can, otherwise your understanding of the context will fall short.

JESUS IS BETTER THAN ANGELS (1-2)

In Chapter 1 the author displays Jesus as being perfect. He lists seven reasons why he is better from the get-go and we know that the number seven symbolizes divine perfection. List those seven things below:

1. Heb 1:2b

2. Heb 1:2c

3. Heb 1:3a

4. Heb 1:3b

5. Heb 1:3c

6. Heb 1:4a

7. Heb 1:4b

Jesus is better than angels. What does that mean? It means that Jesus is a much better messenger between God and man than anything they had experienced in the past. Jews relied heavily on interaction with angels in order to know the heart of the Father. But we have the heart of the Father in human form, Jesus, giving us the opportunity to align our hearts with his. Also, as much as some of them may want to be as great as God Himself (for example, Satan), angels are not and will never be like God. But Jesus was.

What other characteristics make Jesus better than angels? (Heb 2:9-18)

to strive after. Many times Moses was seen as being interchangeable with the Law because he was the one that received it from God.

Describe Moses in five words below:

1.

2.

3.

4.

5.

How else is Jesus better than Moses? (Heb 3:1-6)

JESUS IS BETTER THAN MOSES AND JOSHUA (3-4)

Next up, the author looks at Jesus as being better than Moses and Joshua, with the main focus on Moses.

Moses was the be all and end all in Judaism. All Jews look to him as the definition of holiness and the image

JESUS IS BETTER

Throughout this book, the author includes five perils (or warnings) for the reader, that explain what will happen if they fall away from their faith. We find one of the warnings in Hebrews 3:7-19.

After reading those verses, how would you define unbelief? What are some ways that you can help each other to continue believing?

Who was Melchizedek again? (Gen 14:18-20)

No matter if you believe Melchizedek was actually Jesus himself or not, he was definitely a "type" of Christ. A "type" is an Old Testament illustration of the coming King.

What are some other "types" of Christ in the Old Testament?

JESUS IS BETTER THAN THE AARONIC PRIESTHOOD (5-7)

The Old Testament is great for discovering what types of leadership did and did not work for the Israelites. When it all came down to it, none of the types of leadership that the people desired ended up working right. They tried the leadership of prophets, kings, and priests individually, but what they really needed was someone who could hold all three spots.

The author brings up our good friend Melchizedek. As we've discussed, he represents one of the great mysteries of the Bible.

The Aaronic priesthood was birthed out of the holiness that was required under the Law. The Law was something to measure holiness against and, in reality, just showed the people that a holy life was impossible without a savior. Even though the Israelites had no way out, their hope was to remain in their future Messiah. Until the Messiah came, life was going to be very difficult.

The coming of Christ erased the need for the priesthood because whereas the Law brought death, Christ brought life and life abundantly. Hallelujah!

What are some other ways that Jesus is better than the Aaronic priesthood? (Heb 4:14-5:10)

The Old Covenant never worked because it was never God's original intention. People couldn't live up to the 613 laws that they were called to obey. They wanted to live a life that mimicked the surrounding societies and peer pressure played a major influence. Time after time God gave them what they wanted, but it was never enough. The Law and God's involvement wasn't the issue. It was their selfish desires and pride that made them stumble. They needed a foolproof way to be right with God. They needed Him to perform something miraculous. They needed a new covenant and a new nature.

So what did this New Covenant of Jesus allow them to do?

JESUS IS BETTER THAN THE OLD COVENANT (8-10)

How were people in the Old Covenant judged and saved vs. in the New Covenant?

What does this new inheritance mean for our lives?

PERSEVERANCE IS KEY (11-12)

Chapter 11 of Hebrews is an unbelievable chapter that displays what many call the "Great Hall of Faith". It's an overview of the most faithful people in Israel's history, including Abraham, Sarah, Jacob, Moses, Rahab, and others. These are the people that set the bar and who we should be looking up to as believers.

Who is your role model in Hebrews 11? What can you pull from their life as motivation to grow in your faith?

Living by faith is a lifestyle that we, as believers, should daily strive for. It isn't easy because the devil does a great job of scaring us out of it, but let me tell you, walking by faith is FAR more enjoyable than running from it. We serve a powerful God, and He chose to make his home inside of us. The least we can do is let Him work through us.

On a scale of 1-10, where would you put your faith?
1 being "I am a realist and don't think that God can use me to do the impossible".
10 being "If God says 'Jump', I JUMP".
What's holding you back from having greater faith?
(see Matt 9:24 for encouragement!)

Having great faith doesn't come easy. We can believe what we want all day, but when it comes to acting upon our beliefs (aka stepping out in faith), it can be much easier just to keep silent. Many times acting upon our faith can be squashed because of a fear of man in our lives. I've struggled with that for a long time, especially when it comes to, for example, praying for an unbeliever or laying hands on someone and praying for healing.

FINAL THOUGHTS

The author of Hebrews makes it clear that focusing on religion will get you nowhere, while accepting the redemptive work of Jesus will give you eternal life and an abundant one here and now. Our job is to act in faith in response to what God calls us to do. Nothing in life can compare to having the Creator of the universe on your team so we might as well take advantage of it and live life to the fullest.

Make a plan of attack below for how you can better walk out your faith from here on out:

AUTHOR

The author of this epistle is James, the brother of Jesus.

DATE

There are two highly disputed timeframes for when the book of James was actually written:

The first view is the "early view," which says that James was written around AD 47-48, before the Jerusalem Council took place. Hence the reason for not using any of the content from the Jerusalem Council when disputing such relevant topics.

The second view is the "late view," which says that James was written around AD 60-62, after the Jerusalem Council. This view would be taken if James was clarifying various misinterpretations of Paul's word.

AUDIENCE

James wrote to all of the Jews that were scattered at the Dispersion which followed Stephen's death in Acts 8. It was a circulatory letter (meaning it was meant to be circulated); not addressed to a specific location.

REASON

James wrote to explain what fruit should be produced when we live an obedient Christian life and he also stressed the need for widsom from above.

THEME

Faith, Works, and Wisdom

KEY VERSE

"So also faith by itself, if it does not have works, is dead. But someone will say, 'you have faith and I have works.' Show me your faith apart from your works, and I will show you my faith by my works." (2:17-18 ESV)

JAMES

THE BOOK

SECTIONS

Trials and Testing (Ch 1), Faith and Works (Ch 2), The Tongue and Wisdom (Ch 3), Worldliness (Ch 4), Wealth and Patience (Ch 5)

KEY WORDS

Faith, Works, Law, Wisdom

The book of James is known as the "Proverbs of the New Testament". It's called "Wisdom Literature", which means it is packed with content on how to live your life as a Christian. It's the least doctrinal type of writing, but it is the most practical for day-to-day living.

The five main topics that James looks into are:

Trials

Faith and Works

The Tongue

Wisdom

Wealth

Wisdom Literature doesn't typically follow an outline. James goes back and forth between topics with no reasoning behind it. We are going to touch on the five main topics and see how they can each relate to today.

Trials:

The first topic is trials and tribulations. Something Christians know a lot about. As we have looked at before, and will continue to see, being a new creation means that you are no longer "worldly". You now belong to the kingdom of heaven instead of the earth. Spiritual warfare tends to ramp up heavily when you begin walking in your new identity as a child of God which creates trials and tribulations in your day-to-day life.

A great description that many believers use is that we are "in the world, but not of it". Our true home is in heaven now, making this earthly sod just a pit-stop on the way home.

What are some ways that you can be a light in this dark world?

One thing to realize when dealing with trials or spiritual warfare or persecution is that God may test you, but it is always Satan who tempts you. Testing is a way for you to grow in your faith, while tempting is done in hopes of making you fail.

Can you remember any times of great testing in your life? What about tempting?

In the Old Testament, God allowed Satan to TEST Job's faith in Him because He knew that Job was a faithful servant. Job was not given more than he could handle. So no matter what trial or tribulation you are put through, always keep your focus on Christ and allow Him to make you stronger in your faith.

Faith and Works:

James approaches the topic of faith and works in a way that we do not see anywhere else in the Bible. Paul always taught that salvation is through grace alone, not works. James seems to be contradicting him. The thing is, Paul was talking about works from the Law, not actions and good deeds. It is true that works do not create salvation, but it is also true that faith should result in good works.

After you became a believer, did you notice any change in your actions? If so, what specifically happened?

The Christian faith isn't just about saying that you believe in God...as many churches claim today. The Christian faith is about growth. It's about transformation. It's about sharing the love of Jesus through our actions. James even says that if there isn't any fruit being produced by your life then you should examine your salvation and determine whether or not you are truly saved.

SPEAK LIFE
SPEAK LIFE
SPEAK LIFE
SPEAK LIFE
SPEAK LIFE
SPEAK LIFE
SPEAK LIFE
SPEAK LIFE
SPEAK LIFE

SPEAK LIFE

What type of good deeds could you do tomorrow to bless those around you?

The Tongue:

The tongue is the most powerful part of your entire body. Because of that, it is also the most difficult piece to control.

Can you think of a time when you wish you would have either spoken up or kept your mouth shut? If so, what happened?

Our tongues have influence. Probably way more influence than we would like them to have. So small yet so potent. The Message translation says "By our speech we can ruin the world, turn harmony to chaos, throw mud on a reputation, send the whole world up in smoke and go up in smoke with it, smoke right from the pit of hell" (3:6).

You don't hear much biblical teaching today on the tongue or the power of words, yet so many people struggle in that area. I had/have struggled with it forever. Before going to Australia, words didn't really mean much to me. I would tell everyone that they were the "best", and I was very sarcastic in my sense of humor. I was eventually confronted about it, and God changed my entire perspective on the power of words.

When Proverbs 18:21 says, "Death and life are in the power of the tongue" (ESV) it's true. James couldn't believe that his audience was using the same tongue to speak blessings and curses over people.

We should be a group of people who are speaking truth into other people's lives through encouragement and holding strong to what the Word says about us. Gossip and negativity towards others should never be attached to our reputation whatsoever.

What are some ways that you can discipline yourself to speaking words of life instead of death?

When the Holy Spirit began convicting me about all of this, there were a few people in my life that bugged me like crazy. And that can mess you up! You can just hear their name and instantly think something negative about them. So every time when I started thinking something bad about them, I would thank God for something about them in return. It changed everything. I would definitely suggest giving it a try if you struggle in that area as well.

What would it look like if you focused on practically living out what James is saying here? What if we were known as people who never talk bad about others? What if we spoke words of thankfulness regarding others instead of disgust? Love instead of gossip?

Let's be the generation that destroys the stigma of Christians being judgmental and hypocritical. Let's share the goodness of Christ in our actions and in our words every day. Changing your mindset can change your life.

Wisdom:

Next up, James shows that there are two different kinds of wisdom. One is earthly wisdom, the other is heavenly wisdom. One is from above, the other is from below... right here on earth.

Do you typically use wisdom from above or from below? Are you alright with that?

As we have seen while looking into other books of the Bible, it is important as believers to maintain a heavenly mindset in every situation...even when it is difficult. Having wisdom from above means that you understand the Father's heart and act upon it. It also means that you are focused on prayer and hearing the Lord's perspective on situations. It's all about relationship; not religion.

How do you think we can keep a heavenly mindset during difficult times?

Approaching situations with earthly wisdom is what happens when we rely on our own experience to direct our response. Every one of us has come from a different background that has transformed our way of thinking. For example, some of us are "street smart"; while others are "book smart". James shows that the goal is not to make decisions in the same way as our peers do, but to reach for wisdom from above instead. For that is where the ultimate wisdom lies.

How can you adjust your thinking to have more of a heavenly mindset each and every day?

Wealth:

The fifth topic that James looks at is wealth and the negative impact it can have on us and on the poor. Thanks to social media and the entertainment industry, we are constantly being told what is cool, right and sexy.

Every ad tries to show us what kind of lifestyle we could be living if we just had their product in our lives. Ads try to make us feel as if we are missing out on something if we don't give in and buy the advertised product. But once we buy it, there is always something bigger and better coming along that we will want next. It's a never ending cycle.

What are some ads that have caused you to purchase a product? What made it so appealing?

One thing that I must state is that money is never the problem. I know many believers who are absolutely loaded. It's the love of money that is at the root of all kinds of evil. It's a heart issue.

Since we are extremely wealthy compared to the rest of the world, what are some things that we can do in order to not get caught up in the money trap?

Citizens of the United States of America have a lot of money. As a whole, we are very wealthy. And yet we have a LOT of problems.

The audience that James was writing to also had a lot of problems. Many of which revolved around money. They were ignoring the poor and completely self-centered in their pursuits. Two things that should not characterize us as believers in Jesus. James' audience needed to redirect their money mindset and share the love of Christ with everyone around them, rich or poor.

FINAL THOUGHTS

Out of the five themes that we just looked at it in the book of James, which one would you like to improve on? Why? What are some things that you can do today to begin the improvement process?

AUTHOR

The author of 1 Peter is the man himself, the apostle Peter. Peter was the leader of the twelve dsciples. Jesus changed his name from Simon, which meant "Reed," to Peter, which meant "Rock." Jesus knew that he would be the foundation of the Church. With that said, Peter was the first pastor who founded the church after Jesus ascended to heaven. We know that Peter was Jesus' favorite disciple even though he denied Jesus three times.

DATE

Peter wrote this first letter around AD 64 at the beginning of Nero's persecution of Christians. Who was Nero and what was his deal?

Nero was the Roman Emperor that reigned from AD 54-68. He was an average emperor at the beginning of his reign, but then things took a turn for the worst around AD 64 during the "Great Fire of Rome." The Roman citizens blamed him for starting the fire because they knew he had grand plans for the city. And in order to cover his tracks, he blamed the fire on the Christians. From then on, the persecution ramped up in disgusting ways as Nero did anything to gain popularity.He would torture Christians by crucifying them, using them as entertainment in fights against lions, and most horrifically, soaking them in oil and impaling them on a pole in his garden to be used as a source of light for his dinner parties.

Rome was anything but a pretty sight for Christians. Word was getting out among churches all over the Greco-Roman world so Peter wrote to them in preparation for what was to come. He knew that he would be crucified eventually so this was one of his last forms of contact with them.

AUDIENCE

Peter wrote this letter to the Twelve Tribes of the Dispersion that were spread out all around Asia Minor. Remember, Paul was the missionary to the Gentiles, while Peter was the missionary to the Jews.

REASON

Peter was writing in order to encourage the believers to remain holy in their suffering and to submit to authority in hopes of sharing love and peace.

THEME

Suffer now and be taken care of later.

THE BOOK

KEY VERSE

"And after you have suffered a little while, the God of all grace, who has called you to his eternal glory in Christ, will himself restore, confirm, strengthen, and establish you." (5:10 ESV)

SECTIONS

Our Salvation (Ch 1:1-12), Called to Holiness (Ch 1:13-2:12), Submission (Ch 2:13-3:7), Our Suffering (Ch 3:8-4:11), The Urge for Change (Ch 4:12-5:14)

KEY WORDS

Suffering, Glory, Hope, Salvation

First Peter is a book of persecution and warning for what was to come in the near future. As things get crazier in our world every day and Christians are persecuted more and more, this book is very relevant for us.

As we saw in the Gospels, Jesus always said that there would be persecution and suffering for those who believed in him. Jesus is above any type of persecution though, and we can hold on to that promise until we meet him.

Why do you think Christians are more likely to deal with persecution?

Though persecution may come, Peter also teaches that we have now been born into a royal priesthood. That means we are princes and princesses. We are ROYALTY. So many times we fail to act like it though because we don't want to look conceited. That's garbage. God is saying that you and I are royalty so we need to believe what He says about us! We are a special group. We are a holy nation. Transforming our minds to accept this truth is crucial in understanding our identity.

How can your life reflect this new title?

"YOU ARE A CHOSEN RACE,
A ROYAL PRIESTHOOD,
A HOLY NATION, A PEOPLE
FOR HIS OWN POSSESSION."

1 PETER 2:9

Peter, also brings up the fact that we are the temple of God. We are His dwelling place on earth. He resides inside of us. That means He can now be anywhere that we are. Since God now dwells within His children, we should be cautious about how we treat our bodies. Believers should be fit, joyful, peaceful, and walking in His strength and power.

Peter, makes it clear that suffering is to be expected. It's part of the normal Christian life. But if your foundation is built on Jesus Christ, you will press on and be rewarded greatly later on.

Perseverance in our Christian walk is crucial, especially in a time when society is doing everything that it can to veer us away from the cross. Learning how to submit to authority is one way that we can persevere. We have a job to pray for our governmental leaders whether we agree with their decisions or not. The only time we should stand up against their decisions is when it goes against Scripture. It can be tough to pray for people that we don't agree with, but it can also be one of the most humbling things we can do.

How can we honor our government even when we don't agree with some of their choices?

In 3:18-20 Peter talks about Jesus going down to preach in Hades when he was crucified, in order to give the people of Noah's day a second chance. We know from other places in Scripture that death is final, and we don't get a second chance so this is a one time deal here. Since it was a one-time deal that means we DO NOT get a second chance to believe in Jesus after we die. We have one shot. You either believe and have eternal life or you don't believe and have eternal punishment. Life is far too short to be playing around with eternity. Live wisely, my friends.

Pick one person that you know who is not a believer. Write out a prayer plan for them and how you want to see God move in their life:

FINAL THOUGHTS

Peter, makes it clear throughout this letter that we are to suffer as Christ suffered. Think about the way Christ suffered and remember…no matter what kind of suffering you may experience now, you will be greatly rewarded in heaven for all of eternity. The best is yet to come! Remember what we learned back in Ephesians? We are in a battle every day so of course the enemy is going to attack us. But we are VICTORIOUS in Christ. Put on the armor of God daily so that you can stand firm and fight back with God's weapons such as prayer, faith, love, God's Word and the Holy Spirit.

As relevant as this book is to this time and place, we are told that it is only going to become more and more relevant as time moves forward.

In what ways have you experienced physical, spiritual or mental persecution?

What did you learn from Peter that will help you out next time you deal with persecution?

2 PETER

AUTHOR

The second letter of Peter was also written by the apostle Peter.

DATE

Peter knew that his death was right around the corner because of how bad things had gotten in Rome. He penned this last letter around AD 66.

AUDIENCE

Peter is writing this letter to the same group of people that he did the first time around, the churches in Asia Minor.

REASON

Peter wrote this second letter because false teaching was at an all-time high, and their doctrine was becoming blurred. He didn't want that to happen so he is encouraging them to stick to the truth.

THEME

Watch out for false teachers.

KEY VERSE

"Therefore, dear friends, since you have been forewarned, be on your guard so that you may not be carried away by the error of the lawless and fall from your secure position. But grow in the grace and knowledge of our Lord and Savior Jesus Christ. To him be glory both now and forever! Amen." (Ch 3:17-18 NIV)

SECTIONS

Growth in Truth (Ch 1), False Prophets and Teachers (Ch 2), The Coming of Judgement (Ch 3)

KEY WORDS

False Teachers, Truth, Godliness, Knowledge

THE BOOK

Second Peter has a similar layout to 1 Peter in the sense that it focuses on salvation, warnings, and how to deal with what is ahead. Both letters focus on having a strong foundation so that we will not be shaken.

Through God's promises, Peter says that we can be partakers in the divine nature. Peter doesn't say that we become God, like Buddhism or New Age beliefs may suggest, but we are going from glory to glory. Becoming more like Christ every day.

1:5-7 lists a group of qualities that produce more fruit in our lives and transform us into like-mindedness with Christ. They are:

Diligence, moral excellence, knowledge, self-control, perseverance, godliness, brotherly kindness, and love.

We should be striving to practice these qualities every single day. **What can you do today to increase in each of those qualities? Make a list of what you need to improve on:**

When we get to Jude later on, you will realize that 2 Peter 2 is almost word for word the same as Jude.

Can you think of other places in the Old Testament or New Testament where we see word-for-word similarities? (for example, Jude 6 and 2 Peter 2:4)

If they are so similar, which one do you think was written first?

Whereas the mockers are actually present in Jude, 2 Peter shows that they are still in the future, so Peter most likely wrote first. It can be assumed that the two of them were friends though since Jude was Jesus' brother. The same problems were a part of both of their churches.

Peter and Jude both knew that if there was false teaching in the church then it wouldn't matter how much persecution they received, it would crumble from the inside out. That's why Peter is again emphasizing how important it is to have a strong foundation. If they have a scriptural understanding of salvation, then they will be able to discern between what is true and what is of the enemy.

In 3:3-4, Peter shows that there will be mockers that come against the church's view of the Second Coming. We are experiencing that right now as many people feel that we are getting closer and closer to the Second Coming.

But for some odd reason, many churches today fail to acknowledge the Second Coming in their teachings. But that's what should be our hope for the future!

Even if people mock Jesus' return, Peter says that he hasn't come back yet because he is allowing people more time to be saved. It isn't a bad thing at all. He's slowing it down out of love for humanity. He wants as many people as possible in the Kingdom, but he is giving them the choice. That way their love for him will be pure.

How can you respond to people who make fun of your beliefs or mock you?

While studying through all of the New Testament epistles, we have come across a sense of urgency in gaining believers that has been lost in much of Christianity today. It all comes down to our view of life. If we have an eternal mindset, then it should be our main goal in life to spread the Good News. On the flip side of that, if we are focused on life and how to survive, then we will be slow in sharing the gospel. Your actions all revolve around your mindset.

What are some things that you can do to have more of an eternal mindset in your day to day life?

If we remain focused on the eternal and what is to come, Peter says that it will be much easier to deal with scoffers and false teachers. We are blessed with knowing about the new earth that is right around the corner; they aren't. So it really doesn't matter what they say about you or your beliefs because you know that the trouble they're causing you is temporary. The New Earth will be heaven on earth with no sin or evil anywhere in sight. All will be renewed.

As believers, we are also at an advantage in knowing what is to come. Therefore, our lives should reflect it here and now. It should be our desire to live holy and blameless lives in the power of the Holy Spirit instead of abusing grace by continually choosing to sin. We are representatives of Jesus on earth. That's why he left. So that we could be his representatives EVERYWHERE at the same time. That is why it is so important to know biblical truths about God in order to be good representatives of him. Knowing the Father's heart should be one of our top prayers. We have been charged with a mission. Let's do it right!

All in all, 1 and 2 Peter are both very relevant to us today. We learned that our foundations must include faith, hope and love, in order to deal with the persecution and false teaching that is coming at us. We must keep our eyes on Jesus and do our best to mimic his every move here on earth. Life is short. Use it wisely.

SONSHINE

FINAL THOUGHTS

When I studied 2 Peter for the first time I thought that it was a book I couldn't really relate to. When Peter talked about false teachers that didn't click with me whatsoever because I didn't think that was an issue in the Church today…at all.

Then I began to study some of the beliefs of various current denominations, and I was shocked to realize that there is false teaching going on EVERYWHERE. I am blown away by how unbiblical some teachings are, yet people believe it because they don't know the Bible for themselves.

Well guess what:
The belief that you must repent through another person is NOT biblical.
The belief that miracles no longer happen is NOT biblical.
The belief that the Holy Spirit is no longer relevant is NOT biblical.
The belief that child baptism covers you for life is NOT biblical.

There are many things taught in some churches today that are just flat out lies, but you wouldn't know that unless you knew the truth. That's why I am so proud of you for taking the time to dive into the Word this year and learn for yourself what is and what is not of God. We have the two greatest gifts in the world available 24/7: The Holy Spirit and the Bible. Don't let a day slip away without taking advantage of each of them.

Spend some time in prayer this week thanking God for providing you with the desire to study His Word. Also, ask Him to open your eyes to see what is from Him and what is a lie that has masqueraded as truth in your life.

LETTERS OF JOHN

AUTHOR

The apostle John wrote all three letters at the end of his 30-year residence in Ephesus.

DATE

These three letters were written before his death in AD 98 and after he wrote his Gospel, making it around AD 90-95.

AUDIENCE

John's first letter was written to the churches in Asia Minor, surrounding where he lived in Ephesus. He had an amazing relationship with all of churches after being there for 30 years, and they were all in true fellowship with one another.

REASON

John wrote this first letter to focus even more on fellowship within their communities, to teach them more about sin, to confirm their salvation and to discredit any false teaching that was infiltrating the area.

THEME

Security in eternal life.

KEY VERSE

"I will write these things to you who believe in the name of the Son of God that you may have eternal life." (5:13 ESV)

SECTIONS

Walk Out Light (Ch 1-2), Walk Out Love (Ch 3-4), Walk Out Confidence (Ch 5)

KEY WORDS

Fellowship, Sin, Light, Love, Truth

THE BOOK

As is apparent in this letter, John sees things in a very black and white manner. Everything in life falls into one of two categories: Good or Evil. You are influenced by both and can choose which one you want to focus on.

Just as we saw in the Gospel of John and will see again in Revelation, John always writes in sevens. He knows the divine importance of the number and follows that structure throughout his main points.

In this letter, he has seven main contrasts that he looks at:
- Light and Darkness
- Truth and Lies
- Loving the Father and Loving the World
- Life and Death
- Children of God and Children of the Devil
- Love and Hate
- Good Works and Bad Works

Side Note: There are quite a few modern songs sprouted out of the verses in this letter. See how many you can pick up on.

What happens to darkness when you flip on a light? Good job. It disappears.

The same is with Christ. We know that he IS light and since he is inside of us then we too, are light. That is a profound revelation to have. That means whenever we go into a "dark" area, it is no longer dark because we are there. Christ in us exposes the darkness and makes it disappear. Having that realization should develop confidence next time you are in a place that lacks the presence of God. We can overpower any tactic the enemy uses against us based on Jesus' shed blood and who we are in Christ. That's amazing stuff right there.

Does that change how you view darkness?

John, goes on to tell the audience to love the Father and not the world, meaning the world system. The world is full of lust, pride, greed and unrighteousness, while the "world" of the Father is full of life, light, love, joy, peace, goodness, etc. We are given a choice to decide which one will direct our actions. Obviously the right answer for us is to walk in our true citizenship of heaven. When we walk in the "world" of our Father instead of the world around us, that is when heaven really does come to earth. It is never easy though. The opposition from this world is strong and will always put up a fight against anything that goes against the norm. Opposition in this world is a given for God's children, but we can be confident and bold because Christ is in us and goes with us.

What does it mean to you to be a citizen of heaven while here on earth?

John then dives into a topic that is highly debated and seems to contradict many teachings within the Church today. In 3:9, John says that if you are born of God then you cannot sin. I don't know about you, but I can definitely still sin.

What are your thoughts on this statement before we look at it more?

The issue here is about living in sin and practicing sin even when you know it's wrong. The life of a Christian is about this process called sanctification, which we explored in Galatians. It's the work that the Holy Spirit does in our lives internally.

When I decided to start pursuing Christ with all of my heart, He had some serious cleaning up to do. I felt like a punching bag, getting swung at left and right in order to change my thoughts and desires personally, professionally, and relationally. I admit that I still struggle with changing, but the intensity of the battle has decreased as I have become more and more like Jesus.

That's what John is getting at. The closer you get to Christ; the less that sin will have an impact on your day. Our desire should be to become more Christ-like. If you are truly pursuing Him then there should be visible signs of progress being made.

What has the Holy Spirit called you to give up during your sanctification process?

Everything in life for a believer comes down to four letters: LOVE. Love for God and love for others. That should be the motive behind everything that we do. Paul also preached heavily on that love in 1 Corinthians 13. John, in 3:18, says that we are to love in deed and truth, not word and tongue.

What are some ways to love in deed and truth?

As a new creation, walking by the Spirit, it is not natural for us to sin anymore. The seed of God inside of us contradicts with the influence of the devil on the outside of us. Sin is no joke and God doesn't take it lightly. We must redirect our focus to allow Him to do work inside of us and be used for His greater purpose.

Verse 3:8b says, "The reason the Son of God appeared was to destroy the works of the devil" (ESV). With Christ in us that is one of our purposes today. In our job. At our school. In our love life. No matter the situation, we are also called to destroy the works of the devil.

In what ways can you destroy the works of the devil?

DARK
LIES
EVIL
LOVE WORLD
BAD WORKS
FLESH
HATE

LIGHT
TRUTH
GOOD
LOVE FATHER
GOOD WORKS
SPIRIT
LOVE

John makes the statement that "God is love". I actually have that tattooed on my forearm, but I didn't really understand what it meant until a year after I got it.

What do you think "God is love" means?

John doesn't say "God loves", he says that God IS love. God can only BE love. In the case of Christianity, we know that He is the Father, Son, and Holy Spirit, all in one. In perfect harmony. In loving nature. The definition of love. There is no judgment between them, no jealousy, no pride, nothing. The Trinity moves in the essence of love.

God thought that the love was so good that He wanted to share it with others because He is selfless. That's why we were created in the first place. So that humanity could also share in the love of God. And when you know the true love of the Father, you understand why He wanted to share it. That's exactly what John is telling us to do: Share it.

John wants us to have confidence in our new nature. We are now living on the opposite side of the spectrum compared to what we used to know. Life really might be just as black and white as John makes it. There's good and evil. Pick a side.

Moving forward, 2 and 3 John are small, nearly identical letters that are written to a man and a woman. Both needed to be written from a different angle in order to adapt the different way that men and women think. The main issue for both was the topic of hospitality.

SECOND LETTER

AUDIENCE

The audience of 2 John is widely debated because he does not specify who the "elect lady and her children" are. That leaves it up to you to decide between the three main options that I have heard:

First, John could be writing to an unknown woman who has her own house church, most likely in Ephesus.

Second, John could be writing to a church as a whole and its members. The "elect lady" would be the church itself, her "children" could be the members, and her "sister" could be another church.

Third, which is rarely taught but makes the most sense to me, is that John was writing to Mary, the mother of Jesus. Mary would have been known as an "elect lady" considering she was the mother of Jesus Christ. We know that she had other children and a sister. Also, John was told by Jesus to look after her, which would go in line with the topic of this letter.

But we don't know for sure and quite frankly, it isn't that important.

REASON

John writes to her as a warning against showing hospitality to false teachers.

THEME

Hospitality

KEY VERSE

"If anyone comes to you and does not bring this teaching, do not receive him into your house or give him any greeting." (10 ESV)

SECTIONS

Love Others (Ch 1-6), Be Cautious (Ch 7-13)

KEY WORDS

Love, Abide, Antichrist, Teaching

THIRD LETTER

AUDIENCE

John wrote his third letter to a man named Gaius who had a house church somewhere in Asia Minor.

REASON

John wrote to encourage Gaius in his love for hospitality, to deal with the pride of Diotrephes and to tell them to accept the teaching of Demetrius.

THEME

Be accepting of other believers.

KEY VERSE

"Therefore we ought to support people like these, that we may be fellow workers for the truth." (8 ESV)

SECTIONS

To Gaius (Ch 1-8), To Diotrephes (Ch 9-10), About Demetrius (Ch 11-14)

KEY WORDS

Truth, Testimony, Good, Evil

THE BOOKS

These two letters by John are small and fairly self-explanatory. He is telling the two recipients how to be better at showing hospitality. The woman needed to be more cautious and the man needed to be more open.

There were many missionaries going around in the Greco-Roman world, and they were dependent on the hospitality of other believers. That situation allowed for false teaching to spread because anybody that was a "believer" was accepted.

Who is the most hospitable person that you know? Why?

In the third letter, John calls out Diotrephes for being too prideful about accepting other teachings. He thought it was his way or the highway and was not showing hospitality to anybody that came to his door. John was disappointed because the church was then missing out on great truths and testimony. One of those testimonies was that of Demetrius so John charges them to pay attention to him.

Well there you have it. Both letters are short and right to the point.

How can you be more hospitable to other believers?

FINAL THOUGHTS

Pick an action that we looked at in the preceding pages that you would like to grow in the most: Being light, loving the Father, not practicing sin, loving others or being hospitable.

Now put together a POA (Plan-Of-Attack) for how you will grow in that topic over the next month or two below.

Example:

I want to focus on becoming more holy (not practicing sin) over the next few months.

- In order to do so, I am going to spend 30 minutes in a quiet time every morning, praying and meditating on Scripture.
- One of my prayers will be, "Lord, make me holy as you are holy. Whatever that looks like on my part. Sanctify me".
- Also, every time that I do deliberately sin, I am going to align my heart with the Father's immediately to raise my awareness of sinning in the first place.

AUTHOR

The author of Jude is "Jude, a servant of Jesus Christ and brother of James" (1:1 ESV). That would make both Jude and James half-brothers of Jesus.

DATE

Jude was written shortly after 2 Peter, but before the destruction of the temple in AD 70, making it between AD 67-69.

AUDIENCE

Jude most likely wrote to believers from the Dispersion who were possibly located in Antioch since it was a hub and easily accessible for false teachers.

REASON

Jude wrote because false teachers were influencing the church and causing believers to stray away. Jude is encouraging them to stay strong and fight for their faith.

THEME

Contend for the faith.

KEY VERSE

"Beloved, although I was very eager to write to you about our common salvation, I found it necessary to write appealing to you to contend for the faith that was once for all delivered to the saints." (3 ESV)

SECTIONS

Denouncing False Teachers (Ch 1-16), The Proper Response (Ch 17-25)

KEY WORDS

Contend, False Teachers, Ungodly, Godliness, Judgement

THE BOOK

Jude is a book that many people skip over because they don't understand the importance of it. Honestly, it is a pretty strange one. If you compare it to 2 Peter 2, it's almost the same letter, too. Jude addresses a few problems that the audience is facing, which all began with a group of false teachers.

First off, the false teachers were teaching that you could abuse grace. They were saying that once you were saved you could sin all you wanted to and it didn't matter. That's not the Father's heart at all. Yes, grace covers us when we mess up, but our lifestyle should no longer reflect a life of sin. We are new creations and have the power inside of us to live righteously; to go from glory to glory.

Secondly, the false teachers were teaching that Jesus was not the ONLY way to Heaven, but just ONE of the ways. I don't need to explain that one. You know Jesus is the only way (John 14:6).

Which scriptures would you use to combat those false teachings?

Jude compares what is happening with these churches to Israel with the golden calf in the wilderness, Nephilim and Sodom & Gomorrah. **Can you recall what happened in all of those instances?**

Golden Calf: (Ex 32)

Nephilim: (Gen 6:4)

Sodom & Gomorrah: (Gen 19)

Jude also mentions three people that the Christians will be transformed into if they keep listening to the false teachers. He uses Cain, Balaam, and Korah as examples. **Do you remember what those three people did?**

Cain: (Gen 4)

Balaam: (Num 22, 31:6; 2 Pet 2:15)

Korah: (Num 16)

The situation was crumbling and Jude makes it clear that they need to change their ways quickly, otherwise they would crash and burn. Jude truly cared about their salvation and knew what would happen to them if they didn't stick to the truth.

How would you deal with false teachers in your church today?

The sole focus needs to be on following Scripture and modeling the Father's heart towards those who have been deceived. That means approaching the situation in a loving, yet firm manner. We need to make the truth known, but our actions must flow from a heart of love.

Jude begins characterizing the false teachers as "godless". He actually uses that word four times in two verses to describe them. Their godlessness was a mockery of godliness. Talk about a fitting topic! The church today is constantly being mocked by our culture for its godliness. We have become the brunt of society's jokes. God tells us in His Word that this would happen though so we can't be too surprised or get too upset when it does.

The one thing that Jude makes clear is that we are to contend for the gospel. We must fight and stand up for the truth. Jesus is the way, the truth, and the life. Nobody comes to the Father except through him. No matter what your peers say, if you remain focused on your relationship with Jesus, then you will always be taken care of.

FINAL THOUGHTS

Jude teaches us that we must learn how to contend for the faith. As things get crazier and crazier in the world, the lines between good and evil are only going to get pushed farther and farther apart. We need to be prepared to stand up for the truth no matter what comes at us.

One way to contend for the faith is by memorizing Scripture, holding on to those truths, and sharing them with others. I would encourage you to begin memorizing Scripture if you don't already. Knowing what God says about Himself and about you will serve as great reminders when things begin to heat up. You will find a few of my favorite verses below, as well as room for you to write your own.

"Now all glory to God, who is able, through his mighty power at work within us, to accomplish infinitely more than we might ask or think." (Ephesians 3:20 NLT)

"And we know that in all things God works for the good of those who love Him, who have been called according to His purpose." (Romans 8:28 NIV)

"He himself bore our sins in his body on the tree, that we might die to sin and live to righteousness. By his wounds you have been healed." (1 Peter 2:24 ESV)

"Set your mind on the things above, not on the things that are on earth. For you have died and your life is hidden with Christ in God." (Colossians 3:2-3 NASB)

"Whatever you ask in prayer, believe that you have received it, and it will be yours." (Mark 11:24 ESV)

"For God so loved the world that He gave His one and only Son, that whoever believes in Him shall not parish but have eternal life." (John 3:16 NIV)

REVELATION

AUTHOR

The author of Revelation is the apostle John, along with the Gospel of John and his three Epistles.

DATE

Revelation was written towards the end of John's life and after his other writings, making it sometime in the mid-90's AD.

AUDIENCE

According to Revelation 1:11, John is writing this book to the "seven churches, to Ephesus and to Smyrna and to Pergamum and to Thyatira and to Sardis and to Philadelphia and to Laodicea."

REASON

John wrote the book of Revelation to show the completion of God's plan.

THEME

The current Church and it's future.

KEY VERSE

"Write therefore the things that you have seen, those that are and those that are to take place after this." (1:19 ESV)

SECTIONS

Past (Ch 1), Present (Ch 2-3), Future (Ch 4-22)

KEY WORDS

Church, Jesus, Judgement, Satan, Nations

THE BOOK

After reading Revelation this week, it wasn't as daunting of a task as people make it seem, was it?

Revelation has a strange stigma attached to it that causes many people to steer clear from ever attempting to read it. Yet it is the only book in the Bible that promises a blessing upon the reader. That's interesting.

How do you feel about Revelation? Why do you think so many people choose not to study it?

Yes, some of the visions may seem weird to us because they aren't the type of thing that we see every day in the natural realm. That's because Revelation is what we call Apocalyptic writing. It looks into the future from the spiritual realm instead of the natural realm perspective. It's the future as God sees it. Revelation completes the story of redemption. We can hold on to the hope for a better tomorrow based on what God's Word says about the future. This is His promise of what will one day be our reality.

Before we look at the text more, let's do a quick little eschatology overview...the two major view of eschatology are Amillennialism and Premillennialism.

Amillennialism is a symbolic interpretation of the Millennium and doesn't believe that Jesus will have a literal 1000-year earthly reign.

Premillennialism is a literal interpretation and holds the view that Jesus will have an earthly reign with a rapture of Christians.

Speaking of the rapture, there are three major views on that as well: Pre-tribulation, mid-tribulation, post-tribulation.

Pre-tribulation believes that there will be a rapture of Christians sometime before tribulation.

Mid-tribulation believes that the rapture will take place halfway through when the antichrist breaks the peace treaty with Israel.

Post-tribulation believes that Christians will live through the tribulation period and be taken away right at the end of the world.

Feel free to research all five views more in-depth online.

Before studying the book of Revelation, did you prescribe to any of the above views on eschatology? If so, which one(s)?

The way that you interpret Revelation plays a major part in your hope for the future and what is yet to come.

Let's go.

As we saw with the key verse, 1:19 gives an overview of the entire book. John is told to "Write therefore the things that you have seen, those that are and those that are to take place after this" (ESV). You will see throughout the book that Chapter 1 is that which he has seen, Chapters 2-3 are the seven churches, which were currently there, and Chapters 4-22 are what is to come after the time of the churches.

In Chapter 1 alone there are 24 titles or descriptions of Jesus Christ. In all of Scripture there are actually 200-some.

What titles of Jesus can you think of?

In Chapters 2 and 3, John is told what to tell the seven main churches in Asia Minor at the time. Not only were the churches dealing with their own issues, but all of the churches showed spiritual issues that the Church as a whole has dealt with throughout history. Some scholars believe that each of the churches mentioned in Revelation represent a different time period in church history, which would most likely place us in the seventh and final church, Laodicea, which deals with lukewarm faith.

The church of Ephesus had left their first love behind.
The church of Smyrna was on the verge of suffering great persecution.
The church of Pergamum was dealing with the influence of false teaching and pagan idolatry.
The church of Thyatira was being led astray by a Jezebel spirit inside the church.
The church of Sardis had become deadened to their faith.
The church of Philadelphia had persevered and held tightly to God's promises.
The church of Laodicea was lukewarm, neither cold nor hot.

John is told to critique each of the churches in order to build them up into the holy church that they were created to be, not to make them discouraged. That's the same today. I used to get offended when people critiqued my work or thinking, but in reality they were just trying to make me a better, holier person.

How do you handle criticism? Can you relate to any of the seven churches? If so, what does John suggest you do regarding that trait?

When we get to Chapter 4, John is now in heaven with all seven of the churches and everyone is in full-on worship mode. John gives us a great vision on what was happening in the throne room and who was present. He introduces us to a group of 24 elders who are both kings and priests and are ruling alongside Christ. We also see the four creatures that we saw both in Ezekiel and Isaiah who have different faces, six wings, and are full of eyes (Ezekiel 1 and Isaiah 6).

Everyone worshiping. Praising the King of Kings.

How does worship currently influence your life?

new

Next up, a scroll with seven seals is given to the Lamb that was slain, representing Christ as the ultimate sacrifice. The angels, creatures, and elders all exalted the Lamb with praise because the time had finally come to jumpstart the beginning of the end…the seal, trumpet, and bowl judgments from Chapters 6-16. Those chapters are very difficult to interpret because it is unclear when each of them will take place. But what we do know is that the judgments get worse as time moves on.

If you condense each judgment and look at them sequentially, it is easier to grasp what John says will happen during the End Times.

The Seven Seals (6:1-17; 8:1-5):
1. The white horse is the Antichrist coming forth
2. The red horse brought major wars
3. The black horse brought famine
4. The pale/green horse brought death
5. The fifth seal displayed all of the martyrs during this time
6. The sixth seal was an earthquake that caused terror throughout the world
7. The seventh seal called for silence in heaven for 30 minutes followed by the seven trumpet judgments

The Seven Trumpets (8:6-13; 11:15-19 and are part of the seventh seal):
1. Fire and hail mixed with blood. 1/3 of the earth and trees were burned up along with all of the grass
2. A massive, flaming rock will be hurled into the sea. 1/3 of the sea became blood because 1/3 of the creatures died and 1/3 of the ships were destroyed
3. Similar to the second trumpet, but hitting the earth's rivers and springs of water. Many men died as a result
4. The sun, moon, and stars were all darkened and daylight was decreased by 1/3
5. Demons unleashed to torment unbelievers for five months
6. A demonic army of 200 million horsemen were released to kill 1/3 of humanity
7. The kingdom of God reigns supreme after a major earthquake and hailstorm, introducing the seven bowl judgments

The Seven Bowls (16:1-21):
1. Sores appear on the flesh of unbelievers
2. Every living thing in the sea dies
3. Rivers and springs of water become blood
4. The sun's heat is turned up, and scorches humanity
5. The kingdom of Satan becomes darker, and the first bowl is intensified
6. Water from the Euphrates is dried up, and the battle of Armageddon takes place
7. There is a major earthquake and a hailstorm

As terrible as all of these things are, it is crucial to remember that God is just in all of His judgments and ways. This judgment period will be the final chance for people to repent of their sins in order to be forgiven and given eternal life in Christ.

7777777
7777777
7777777
7777777
7777777
7777777
7777777

SEVEN
SEVEN
SEVEN
SEVEN
SEVEN
SEVEN
SEVEN

Now that you have studied the entire Bible, how do you justify God's wrath during the End Times even though He is a God of love?

The next pause that we see in the story is in Chapters 10 and 11 between the sixth and seventh trumpets. John is asked to measure the temple, not including the outer court because that will be handed over to the Gentiles for 42 months. He is also told about the two witnesses that will preach throughout the earth and be given authority from God for 1,260 days (aka 42 months or 3 ½ years).

The authority the witnesses have been given allows them to call down fire from heaven, to shut up the sky so that it doesn't rain, to turn the water into blood, and to strike the earth with various plagues.

Which two prophets performed those miracles in the Old Testament? (2 Kings 1:10 and Exodus 5-12) **Although Scripture doesn't tell us, who do you think the two witnesses will be?**

After preaching for 42 months, the Antichrist will finally be given permission to kill the two witnesses. After doing so, he places their bodies in the street so that everyone in the world can see his "power over God". Three and a half days later they rise from the dead and ascend into heaven, giving every witness of this miracle another reason to repent. This is such a great picture of the Father's heart. He truly does want every person to surrender themselves to Him and accept His salvation.

In Chapter 12, John is given a strange vision of a woman who has a male child and a dragon is trying to eat the child. What?!

Let's break it down a little bit:
The woman is an image of Israel, the people of God.
The male child is Jesus.
The dragon is Satan.

Now that we have that understanding, the story makes a lot more sense. It is an entire summary of God's plan of redemption for His people, and it includes the enemy trying to thwart God's plan. It is a vision of the past as well as a prophecy for the future.

During the time of persecution of the woman, the dragon calls on two "beasts" to take over. One from the sea. One from the earth. Both are influenced by Satan for a period of 42 months. They are what are commonly called the Antichrist and the False Prophet. A large amount of deception will come from these two leaders because they will portray themselves as peaceful people. The False Prophet will even be able to perform miracles, tricking many people into believing that he is the Messiah. They will convince people to receive the "mark of the beast", which is a pledge of allegiance to their cause. If you have the mark, you will not be accepted by God or be able to buy/sell anything.

What do you think the mark of the beast will be? Why do you think it is placed on your right arm or forehead?

Next up is the famous Battle of Armageddon that people have been talking about for ages. It is a time when the kings of the south, north, and west all go into battle with each other; only to be attacked by the kings of the east and eventually defeated by Jesus Himself.

Remember the big earthquakes that we saw in the seventh seal, trumpet, and bowl judgments? Chapters 17-18 are about that time. It's the final destruction of Babylon. The entire Bible has been a tale of two cities: Jerusalem and Babylon. We saw the woman that represented Israel in Chapter 12, and now we see the mother of the harlots, which is Babylon. One issue that we see today is that Babylon is no longer a major city...

Do you think Babylon is a literal representation of a physical place today? Or is it all symbolic? If literal, which country could it represent?

In Chapter 17, the woman is shown riding a beast that has seven heads and ten horns. In comparison to the prophecies in Daniel, we know that the horns represent different governments or political figures. The beast is clearly empowered by Satan and will do what is necessary to wipe out Christians and Jews alike. It's the age old battle of good versus evil. God verses Satan. When interpreting this section, things may become clearer if you look at who wants to destroy Christians and Jews.

The battle between good and evil will NOT last forever. Jesus will come down for the second time and take over completely, which also brings up a very controversial part of Scripture: The Millennium and whether or not there will be a physical 1000-year earthly reign of Christ.

According to Scripture, Jesus will come down and reign on earth for 1000 years, from his temple in Jerusalem. After 1000 years, the devil will be released for a short amount of time to try and convert more people to his side. But he will be defeated again in the final battle and sent to hell for eternity. For some reason this teaching has been lost in translation over the years even though it was the view of the early Church.

A literal view of scripture says Jesus will come down and reign on earth for 1000 years, from his temple in Jerusalem. After 1000 years, the devil will be released for a short amount of time to try and convert more people to his side. But he will be defeated again in the final battle and sent to hell for eternity.

Scripture shows us that the Millennial reign will be a time of abundant harvest for everyone, that the Lord will be physically present with us, that sin will still be present and that people will have a choice as to who they want to follow.

When you hear about an "abundant harvest for everyone", what do you think that will look like?

After the Millennium takes place, every unbeliever will be judged for their sin and every believer will be rewarded for their works. Each will go their separate ways for the rest of eternity.

Then it is out with the old and in with the new. God will put the New Heaven and the New Earth in their places and set everything back to His original intent. In communion with God 24/7. Free from sin. Covered in goodness.

What do you think the New Earth will be like? What will we eat? What will we do?

FINAL THOUGHTS

The events which take place during the church age in Revelation are not ones to be taken lightly. They are God's judgment on humanity. We can waste time debating what is actually going to happen and when it will happen or we can see this book as a warning and a book which brings hope.

We know there are ups and there are downs.
Back and forths.
Satan wants to win.
But so does God. And in the end He will.

Seven is the number of perfection. It shows completeness. So, it only seems right that in order to have the perfect ending, the perfect events leading up to it have to take place. Insert the sevens...seven seals, seven trumpets and seven bowls.

Many would state that God's judgment in Revelation is torture for those who didn't follow Him. That is blatantly a false assumption.

God's judgment is an act of love.
It's a second chance.
Amidst judgment, God's granting more time for repentance. For people to fall on their knees before Christ and receive him as Savior and Lord.
God's wrath shows his true heart.

God doesn't want us to spend eternity in hell. He eagerly desires for every single person to spend eternity in the New Heaven and the New Earth. This was His plan all along...it was never for people to suffer eternally. But God loves us and gives us a choice...we can choose him or not. He didn't want us to be robots. But rather He desires a relationship with us. He loves us that much...just look at the cross.

CONCLUSION

THE BIBLE STUDY

THE BIBLE STUDY

CONGRATULATIONS!

You made it! You just accomplished something that most believers have never done - studied the entire Bible, front to back. But YOU did. I am so proud of you, and I know that God is, too.

Before we say our "goodbyes" there is one final thing that I would like you to do - use the rest of this page to explain the Gospel message in an easy-to-understand way that you can use in the future for evangelism.

Matthew 28:19 says, "Go therefore and make disciples of all nations, baptizing them in the name of the Father and of the Son and of the Holy Spirit" (ESV). Now that you know the Word so well, go and share it! Make disciples! Spread the LOVE of our Father!

May God bless you all. -Z

SUNDAY.
SUNDAY.
SUNDAY.
SUNDAY.
SUNDAY.

BEST
DAY
OF THE
WEEK

FAITH SAYS

HOLD ON

—

WHEN DOUBT SAYS

LET GO

FAITH SAYS

HOLD ON

—

WHEN DOUBT SAYS

LET GO

THE
BIBLE
IS
GOOD
FOR
YOU

THE
BIBLE
IS
GOOD
FOR
YOU

NO OTHER NAME

—

JESUS
JESUS
JESUS
JESUS

NO OTHER NAME

JESUS

ABOUT

THE AUTHOR

THE AUTHOR

Zach Windahl is an entrepreneur who loves helping others realize their identity and encouraging them to chase their dreams. Zach grew up a Christian, but in 2014 he went on a journey to Australia in search of the God of the Bible. He needed his stagnant faith to become real. God showed up and completely transformed Zach's life. He splits his time between Minneapolis, Minnesota and south Florida.